P9-CQG-573

301 GREAT

MANAGEMENT IDEAS

from America's
Most Innovative Small Companies

INTRODUCTION BY TOM PETERS

EDITED BY LESLIE BROKAW
FOREWORD BY BRADFORD W. KETCHUM, JR.

Inc.
® MAGAZINE

Copyright © 1995 Goldhirsh Group, Inc.
Boston, MA
All rights reserved.
Printed in the United States of America.

No part of this book may be used or repro-
duced in any manner whatsoever without
written permission except in the case of brief
quotations embodied in critical articles and
reviews. For information, write *Inc.*
Publishing, Attn: Permissions Manager,
38 Commercial Wharf,
Boston, MA 02110-3883.

Book design by Cynthia M. Davis/Cambridge
Prepress. Original design by Robert Lesser.

Portions of this book were originally published in *Inc.* magazine. For information about
purchasing back issues of *Inc.* magazine,
please call 617-248-8426.

This publication is designed to provide accurate and authoritative information in regard to
the subject matter covered. It is sold with the
understanding that the publisher is not engag-
ing in rendering legal, accounting, or other
professional service. If legal advice or other
expert assistance is required, the services of a
competent professional should be sought.

ISBN 1-880394-21-9

First Edition

2 3 4 5 6 7 8 9 10

301 GREAT MANAGEMENT IDEAS

I.
SALES AND MARKETING p. 15

• Advertising • Competition • Direct Sales
• Going Global • Internet
• Market Research • Materials
• Motivating Salespeople • Partnering
• Pricing • Public Relations

II.
CUSTOMER RELATIONS p. 87

• Collections • Communication
• Complaints

III.
MANAGING PEOPLE p. 115

• Benefits • Communication
• Compensation • Firing • Hiring
• Incentives • Motivation • Profit Sharing
• Scheduling • Training

IV.
MANAGING MONEY p. 181

• Banking • Cash Flow • Collections
• Cost Control • Equity • Going Public
• Investor Relations • Mergers • Raising Capital
• Selling the Company • Taxes

V.
PLANNING p. 223

• Advisers • Boards
• Communication
• Education • Ideas
• Meetings
• Strategizing

VI.
SUPPLIER RELATIONS p. 251

• Alliances • Evaluating
• Finance

VII.
OPERATIONS p. 259

• Computers • Cost Control
• Home Office • Insurance • Legal
• Office • Quality Improvements
• Retail

VIII.
BEYOND BUSINESS p. 317

• Community • Family • Giving
• Lifestyle • Partnerships
• Time Management

INDEX p. 344

Over half the ideas in this revised edition of *301 Great Management Ideas* are new to this book. Drawn from the pages of *Inc.* from the last several years, many cover topics that were uncommon when the first edition of *301* came out in 1991—dealing with telecommuting workers, marketing through the Internet, staying in touch with global distributors via E-mail. Other new entries touch on the latest ways that company owners are dealing with the always-changing worlds of banking, finance, and insurance, and with the expanding expectations of today's workers.

Excerpting the recent material for this edition was easy; updating and revising the information from the original book, however, was more daunting. Company names and locations change; some businesses drop off the screen. Mega-thanks to reporter Karen Carney, who did the bulk of that work. She made valuable suggestions for improving the text, and her careful and thorough work was pivotal to this project.

Thanks also to: copyeditor Judith Maas, who also provided extensive reworking of the text to make the information clearer and more concise; the staff of *Inc.* Business Resources, including Hilary Glazer, Mary Ellen Mullaney, and Jan Spiro, for their able and cheerful oversight of the project; designer and creative director Cynthia M. Davis, for her discerning reworking of the book's look; the editor of the original edition, Sara Noble, who first ran with the idea of collecting the best from *Inc.*; designers Robert Lesser and Brady & Paul Communications, for their original book design; the executive editor of this project, Bradford W. Ketchum, Jr., for his wisdom throughout the process and careful editing at the end of it; and *Inc.* editor at large Jeffrey Seglin, who knows everyone and everything.

Big thanks to the company managers who shared their time and experiences with *Inc.*'s reporters and with the world at large.

Biggest thanks to the original reporters, writers, and editors of the material: Margherita Altobelli, Christopher Bergonzi, Alessandra Bianchi, Bo Burlingham, Christopher Caggiano, Karen Carney, John Case, Elizabeth Conlin, Michael Cronin, Susan Donovan, Tom Ehrenfeld, Donna Fenn, Jay Finegan, Jill Andresky Fraser, David Freedman, Elyse Friedman, Robina Gangemi, George Gendron, Vera Gibbons, Susan Greco, Stephanie Gruner, Phaedra Hise, Michael Hopkins, Joshua Hyatt, John Kerr, Joel Kotkin, Nancy Lyons, Joshua Macht, Robert Mamis, Martha Mangelsdorf, Anne Murphy, Bruce Posner, Teri Lammers Prior, Jeffrey Seglin, Brac Selph, Cheryl Sheldone, Ellyn Spragins, Edward Welles, David Whitford, and Stephanie Zacharek.

—*Leslie Brokaw*
Editor
Boston, Massachusetts

A CAST OF TRUE PERFORMERS

Consider this book a 348-page suggestion box, filled with proven management ideas from more than 260 companies in 37 states. Drawn from the pages of *Inc.* and *Inc. Technology* magazines, the ideas have been updated and edited to fit a handbook format. Most of the items originally appeared in a monthly *Inc.* feature called "Hands On," which focuses on managing and growing a business with little or no resources. While their sources and applications vary widely, the 301 ideas have one thing in common: they have been fully tested by the entrepreneurs who generated them. In short, they *work*.

The book is divided into eight chapters, each representing a key discipline for successfully running a small business. Whether you're seeking a solution to a knotty problem or you're simply trying to find a better way of doing things, each chapter offers a collection of mini-cases that will provide a practical answer—or two.

The range of ideas and enterprises is itself inspirational. Digging into the "suggestion box" at random, you'll discover nuggets such as these:

- A Louisiana medical supply CEO who developed a "one-minute sales pitch" for the inaccessible professionals he targets for 15 to 20 cold calls a day.
- A Virginia computer maker that bases a portion of its sales compensation on customer evaluations.
- An Idaho electronic parts manufacturer that set up a "core-customer complaint form" and corrective team to minimize the number of disgruntled accounts.
- A Pennsylvania cafe-restaurant that found a way to computerize its chef's handwriting for daily production of its unique menus.
- A North Dakota apparel chain that builds its customer database daily.
- An Illinois mail-order house that devised a fax-on-demand program to answer customers' technical questions.

A CAST OF TRUE PERFORMERS

- A Vermont bakery that uses a daily scorecard to remind every employee that profits and bread have one thing in common: both should rise.
- A Colorado auto-parts distributor that tapped government programs to get free land for expansion and save $500,000.
- A Texas shoe retailer that uses CD-ROM to minimize checkout time.

From such a sampling, the script for *301 Great Management Ideas* becomes obvious. It is supported by a cast of true performers who are out there running successful enterprises. If there's a single moral to their stories, it's that small-company owners and managers are invaluable sources of help when it comes to inventing clever ways to manage a growing business.

—*Bradford W. Ketchum, Jr.*
Editorial Director
Inc. *Business Resources*
Boston, Massachusetts

**BY
TOM
PETERS**

Thanks to a crazy lifestyle and an overlooked schedule conflict, I once had to take a private charter aircraft from Toronto to Glens Falls, N.Y. More or less.

Fifteen minutes out of Toronto, smoke began to fill the cabin. The cautious pilot (the best kind) made an emergency landing in Buffalo—it seemed as though half the city's fire brigade, not to mention TV "anchors," met us.

Aircraft are phenomenally complex. Frankly, I'm surprised that such problems don't occur more frequently. In any event, though I don't know where any blame should be assigned, I'm not upset by the incident; it's the price of doing business on the run.

But let me tell you, I'm still fuming years later about a full-fare, first-class American Airlines flight from Chicago to San Francisco—where "catering" didn't even include a second bag of peanuts!

Nuts, I say! (And said on TV.)

A brush with death (to overstate only a bit)—I can handle that. But "no peanuts" is intolerable; the memory does—and will—linger on.

"God is in the details." "Retail is detail." There are a hundred like statements. We nod. "Yup." But then, when we come across a Walt Disney or a Sewell Village Cadillac (yes, the "usual suspects"—but that doesn't mean they don't deserve the acclaim), well, then, we know exactly what "passion for detail" is all about.

I've developed a theory over the years, and you'd be hard pressed to dislodge it: the essence of sustainable competitive advantage is 1) the obvious, 2) the little things, and 3) the accumulation of little things over the years.

It turns out that "hard to copy" is easy to copy. And "easy to copy" is hard to copy. Think about it.

A thriving self-serve gas station owner in Northern California is going gangbusters. One of his tricks: he pumps the gas. Hey, you can see it. Why can't the bamboozled competitor across the road "copy" him? (It's been going on for years.) "Beats me," says the puzzled (and successful) station owner.

The "stuff" that comes out of labs—even at a Merck—will be emulated in a couple of years (or less) by a passel of competitors. But a swift process of product development, say, consisting of an attitude of speed and a thousand telling details—that's a very different story.

In short, competitive advantage that sticks is invariably about a hundred, a thousand, a thousand-thousand tiny details—each readily copyable (if taken seriously by competitors, which is unusual and my point), but cumulatively extraordinary in impact and virtually uncopyable in practice. That is, all of the little things consistently done well create a company that defies duplication.

But is this relevant to small business?

You bet! A small business, to be sure, usually one-ups rivals with initial cleverness—a newfangled software spreadsheet, a novel restaurant format. To do so is no small feat. (Most don't get that far.) But today, such cleverness will buy you a year or two of grace at most. The trick—yes, the trick—to sustainability lies, almost entirely, in being obsessed with constant improvement, eventually institutionalizing constant improvement.

Incidentally, I know all too well of what I speak. I run a small business. Our edge, we boast (only to ourselves), is "leading-edge ideas." It may or may not be true, but one thing is sure: a lot of competitors beat us through an absorbing attention to detail. "Dullards," "laggards," we secretly call them—in the same way that Control Data and Sperry called IBM a dull laggard in the 1960s.

Hmmmmm!? Maybe I'd better read this book.

Tom Peters is a consultant, speaker, and best-selling author. His most recent book is The Pursuit of Wow! (*Vintage Books, 1994*).

I

"An entrepreneur knows that a start-up needs to focus on little things. Not the global strategy. Not the Big Plan. A start-up needs cash flow, not a corporate infrastructure. A start-up needs sales staff, not fancy office space and computer systems."

JEFFREY P. SUDIKOFF
founder, chairman, and CEO
of IDB Communications Group,
in Culver City, Calif.

1

IDEA

Low-Cost Take-Home Messages

Whether you call them newsletters, direct-marketing pieces, or miniature catalogs, if you can get material into your customers' hands cheaply, you'll be ahead of the game. One way companies are doing this is to **include a marketing piece with every product**.

Natural Ovens of Manitowoc, in Wisconsin, prints a newsletter on the flip side of its bread labels, which are inserted into each plastic bag along with the bread. The weekly issues include health tips, recipes, and letters from customers. "Thousands of people have called in response to the newsletter," reports Barbara Stitt, co-owner of the bakery, which sells to 1,200 supermarkets. Increasing the label size to fit the newsletter raised costs only half a cent a loaf, while cutting the costs of printing a newsletter separately.

Pete's Brewing, a $33-million microbrewer, in Palo Alto, Calif., tucks into each six-pack of beer a minicatalog touting T-shirts and mugs for sale. The company reports that in the program's first three years, orders to the company's 800 number climbed to 1,700 a month.

2
IDEA

ADVERTISING

Easy Guarantees

Looking for a fresh competitive edge? Maybe your company already has one, and you are just overlooking it. That's what Steve Rondel, president of Advanced Products & Technologies, found.

Observing the mail-room operations of his Redmond, Wash., business, Rondel noticed that very few customers were returning the portable coffee makers, hair dryers, and other travel products his company makes. That's when Rondel realized that **the reliability of his company's products could be a sales feature**. Why not offer a five-year warranty as a way to differentiate Advanced Products from the pack? Given the low return rate, what could it cost?

Virtually nothing, as it turned out. And it's been especially helpful on the company's higher-priced lines. The warranty, says Rondel, lets customers know that his product is worth a premium.

ADVERTISING

Marketing with Competitors

J oining a trade group can be intimidating, and for many entrepreneurs it's an ordeal they'd rather skip. One option: if the existing trade groups don't seem like a good fit, start your own.

In 1993, that's exactly what Dan Burnstein, CEO of Negotiation Pro Co., in Brookline, Mass., did. He founded The Management Software Association (TMSA) to support makers of a new category of management-skills software. Although the members compete with each other, Burnstein says **the advantages of joining together outweigh the negatives**. "We're plugging each other," says Burnstein. "We have 17 people doing PR." That helps every company when potential customers see that the category is part of a growing trend.

One leading software catalog gave TMSA a price break on a full-page ad devoted to members' products. Association members even feature one another's software in their own catalogs and go so far as to swap mailing lists. TMSA also acts as a clearinghouse for journalists in the trade and general press.

The American Society of Association Executives provides free information about starting an association. Call 202-626-2742.

IDEA

• SALES AND MARKETING •

ADVERTISING

Reward Frequent Buyers

Businesses as diverse as coffee shops, dry cleaners, and bookstores have all **adapted the airlines' frequent-flyer concept** to their operations, offering customers a free product or service after they log a certain number of visits.

One twist by a courier company, however, stands out. Instead of offering a free delivery for points earned, the company offers prizes like chocolates and roses. The program targets the administrators, mail clerks, and receptionists who decide which courier to call and who are the key contacts for any delivery service. They accrue points for each delivery and receive monthly statements of point balances along with a four-color flier promoting prizes such as chocolates (30 points) and a dozen roses (15 points).

IDEA

ADVERTISING

When a Product Doesn't Sell

What happens when you produce a product that, as much as you loved it and believed in it, turns out to be a dog? You may be tempted to let the product sit, hoping it eventually will sell. But don't procrastinate. Try everything in your power to get the product off the shelves as quickly as possible.

When any of its 250 products are waning, $62-million Pentech International, a maker of pens and markers, in Edison, N.J., gives retailers a choice: it asks them to either **accept money that can be used to advertise the product** or send the product back at Pentech's expense. "If a product isn't selling, I want it out of there because it's taking up space that can be devoted to another part of my line that moves," says Pentech CEO Norman Melnick. "Besides, having a product languish on the shelves doesn't do much for our image."

Finding an Ad Agency

Homegrown advertising can do a company fine for its first years. It certainly didn't hurt MacTemps, which provides Macintosh-trained temporary workers, for its first four years. But by 1992, the Cambridge, Mass., company was working with more corporate customers, and CEO John Chuang decided that the marketing materials had to keep pace. "Our start-up image looked unprofessional and cheesy," he says.

Because hiring an ad agency would entail a major cost commitment, Chuang **put three months into choosing the right agency**. He drew up a list of 15 agencies culled from *Adweek* and newspaper clippings. He made cold calls to all 15, in each case asking the top account executive about the agency's size and client list and requesting copies of its best print ads. He targeted nine agencies for visits, asking tougher questions: Why were your best print ads effective? Do you know my industry? What is your agency known for? Will I have access to top people?

"We spent half a day at each agency—half that time explaining our business and the other half learning about the agency's background and theory of advertising," says Chuang. In the end, MacTemps signed with a new agency at a reduced retainer and a project fee. Chuang's homework seems to have paid off: not only did the new ads win an award from a temp-services association, but a study by *HR Executive* showed that 25% of readers remembered the ads seven months after seeing them.

7

IDEA

ADVERTISING

Make New Clients News

I n the sea of advertising fliers and promotional materials, it's still possible to remind former and prospective clients that you exist without constantly bugging them. One of the best ways is to **send out cards that announce your business's new clients**.

Every time Alan Gaynor & Co., a Manhattan architecture and interior design firm, gets a new job or completes a major work, it sends out a wedding invitation-sized card to the 1,000-plus names on the company's mailing list. The card names the client and explains what the firm will do or has done for it.

"The card reminds people we're still alive," says Gaynor. "What's more, a builder might learn that we also do interior work, or somebody who has used us on interiors can see we're capable of designing buildings." The company does mailings as often as every two weeks. "It's like advertising," notes Gaynor. "You have to keep sending out the message if you want it to sink in." And Gaynor figures that one new job pays for the cost of two years of mailings.

IDEA

I'll Trade Ya

Television advertising is prohibitively expensive for most small, growing companies. But an audio-video retailer, in Smyrna, Ga., has figured out a clever way to get its name on the air without paying big bucks.

HiFi Buys simply can't compete with national chains' advertising budgets. So it does **a trade with local TV stations**. Whenever HiFi advertises televisions for sale in its newspaper ads, it inserts photos of local TV stations' programs. In exchange, HiFi gets an equivalent amount of advertising on those stations. HiFi's owners figure that in four years of doing the trades, their $60-million business has gotten more than $500,000 worth of free advertising.

IDEA

ADVERTISING

Forgo the Logo

Forget bulls and doughboys—if you're a young company and don't have a corporate logo, you may be better off. That's according to a man who makes his living designing corporate identities, William Drenttel, president of Drenttel Doyle Partners, a New York City design agency. Growing companies shouldn't spend a lot of time—or money—trying to create a symbol they can call their own, he says. "As more and more big companies go about creating or recreating their logos, you're bound to get lost in the clutter," Drenttel observes. A better bet for a small company that wants to work on its image is to pick out a good typeface—clean and classic may be best. But mostly, says Drenttel, "your best bet is to **let your product's name stand for your company**." It's worked for businesses from Oshkosh to Smuckers to Marriott.

10
IDEA

ADVERTISING

Borrow from Other Industries

Sometimes you can really **stand out in one industry just by applying techniques that are standard in another.**

That's what Harvey Mackay learned when he began thinking about how to promote his book *Swim with the Sharks Without Being Eaten Alive.* Mackay had been running Mackay Envelope, in Minneapolis, and simply used all the marketing rules he knew from that competitive business.

Mackay started working on his sales pitch before he even wrote the book, talking with writers, booksellers, and others with publishing experience about how stores get stocked, how important title is, and whether he should bother with illustrations. He got a guarantee from his publisher for a lavish advertising budget, and he spent time with his publisher's representatives and with book buyers to get them excited about pushing his product. Mackay didn't hesitate to ask people he'd met once or twice to endorse the book. "There's no hard sell," he insists. "I just ask them to respond."

"Publishers don't like to be told their business," says Harriet Rubin, an executive editor at Currency/Doubleday, "but Harvey has taught us." In a year, *Sharks* sold some 2.3 million copies.

11
IDEA

COMPETITION

Keeping Tabs on the Joneses

Finding out what your rivals are up to is one of the trickiest tasks of running a business. Most companies gather intelligence by talking to their salespeople and customers and by reading industry publications. Collecting promotional literature and putting competitors to an actual test are ways to expand the scrutiny.

Joe Lethert, president of Performark, a $7-million provider of incentive services, based in Minneapolis, maintains **a library of competitors' materials** so he can quickly compare his prices with those of 8 or 10 competitors, whose catalogs may list from 500 to 5,000 items each. To encourage the sales force to collect rivals' selling materials, Lethert pays his employees $35 for each new piece of competitors' literature they bring in.

When Richard Skeie was CEO of $10-million CE Software Holdings, in West Des Moines, Iowa, he bought the competition's software, tested it, and called rivals' tech support, checking their answers for speed, accuracy, and friendliness.

And Pamela Kelley, founder of $4-million lace-curtain cataloger Rue de France, in Newport, R.I., puts in "tricky, horrible orders" to competitors to see how they handle them.

REAL WORLD

"If we're so weak our competitors can take [our financial] information and use it against us, or our employees can go out and use it to compete with us, then we might as well get out of the business, because we really don't have anything in the first place. People aren't stupid. If you're doing something right and it works, then sooner or later they're going to figure it out and come after you. Can your people respond? Can you keep innovating? Can you stay ahead? These are the real questions you should be dealing with."

KEN HENDRICKS
founder and CEO of ABC Supply, in Beloit, Wis.
ABC Supply ranked number one on the 1986 *Inc.* 500

COMPETITION

The Spoils of War

I f you have a fierce rival in your industry, consider yourself lucky. You can **capitalize on rivalries**, and aggressive companies that target equally combative competitors enjoy a slew of benefits. To get the most out of your competition, do the following:

- Play up the fight in the press. Feisty catfights tend to attract attention, and attention leads to visibility and free press all around. Press coverage can be a market-development subsidy, too, especially if you're in a new industry. Use the rivalry to share the costs of growing the overall industry market.

- Use the "battleground" mentality to rally your employees. Competition can fuel a do-or-die drive to innovate and can be an organizationwide antidote to complacency.

- Use your competitor's successes as benchmarks. At least you'll know when you fall behind or pull ahead.

- Boost your brand by taking a position against your opponent. It's easier to differentiate your stuff when there's somebody else you can call inferior.

IDEA

Mimic the Superstores

I f you run a small retail operation competing against a superstore like Wal-Mart or Kmart, is it better to cultivate a homey feeling at your shop or a "discount" look similar to your rival's?

It may seem counterintuitive, but some small retailers have found that it's more effective to mimic the look and feel of big stores than to highlight their stores' personal nature. With customers accustomed to buying almost exclusively on price, independents say they need to create the perception that they are competitive. "You have to change the box you sell out of and **make your place look like a discount place**," insists Larry Ehmen, co-owner of Fishers Office Plus, in Quincy, Ill.

To update his company's look, Ehmen and his partner, Randy Krutmeier, moved the operation from a 1,600-square-foot store into a 2,500-square-foot retail space and replaced old-fashioned, freestanding display gondolas with shelves of merchandise. "We even painted the ceiling white to make it look less fancy," says Ehmen.

"Now, people come into our store and say, 'Finally, an office discount store.'" The truth is, though, that it was *just* the box that changed; so far, anyway, the prices at Fishers Office Plus have stayed the same.

14
IDEA

COMPETITION

Inside Info on Outside Rivals

Do your employees know enough about your competition? Some companies go out of their way to tell personnel not just about what's going on inside their own company, but also about what's going on outside, in the competitive world.

Newsletters are a good way to pass along industry information. Federal Express newsletters include excerpts of published reports about the Memphis company as well as a "Competitive Corner," with updates on the competition Employee surveys at FedEx show what tabloid editors know instinctively—that stories about the bad guys are among the most popular and best-read items. And even as they provide fun reading, the newsletters help employees become better informed about the industry overall.

15
IDEA

COMPETITION

Taking Stock of Competitors

I f you compete against a publicly traded company, don't overlook the opportunity you have to gain insight into your competitor's operations, financing, and strategy. All you have to do is **become an "insider" by buying a share of your competitor's stock**.

Jim Pierson does that whenever a competitor shows up in the markets served by his company, J.W. Pierson, a wholesaler and retailer of petroleum products, in East Orange, N.J. "I want to keep track of what they're doing," says Pierson, "and the best way is to read their shareholder reports."

The investments pay off, he says. "I can see where they get money, and I get a good idea about their cost structures and acquisition plans." Not that the information has forced Pierson to alter his own plans. Mostly, he says, it broadens his perspective and gives him new clues to work with.

REAL
WORLD

"I consider it the highest
compliment when my
employees go out and start their
own companies in competition
with me. I always send
them a plant to wish them well.
Of course, it's a cactus."

NORMAN BRODSKY
founder and CEO of CitiPostal,
in Brooklyn, N.Y.

16
IDEA

Picking Your Top Targets

I s it worth your time to go after second-tier accounts when what you really want are those first-tier customers? Ken Marshall doesn't think so. CEO of Object Design, a manufacturer of object-oriented databases that was the top-ranking company on the 1994 *Inc.* 500, Marshall credits the company's success to the way it **pursued and aligned itself with name-brand customers.**

When it was starting out, the Burlington, Mass., company carefully aimed for the top five computer-aided-design companies in the country. "Everything we did from a product-development standpoint, from a marketing standpoint, and from our sales-and-distribution network was geared toward bringing our product to those companies," says Marshall. "Rather than sell to the 27th player in the market, we proactively went after those five." The first customer got a great deal, including discounting and free support. "We pretty much said, 'Tell us what you want and we'll do it, as long as you let us use your name,'" says Marshall.

The strategy worked, with Object Design signing on three of the five targets. The company then went after the top companies in other fields, getting AT&T for telecommunications applications, Kodak for computer-aided publishing, Intel for desktop publishing, and IBM for, well, everything. "We were incredibly obnoxious when we started talking to them," says vice-president of marketing, William Blundon, of Object Design's approach to Big Blue. "We treated IBM as an equal, and we were far from that." Object Design turned all those customers into investors as well and now leads its industry in market share, with revenues of nearly $30 million in 1994.

IDEA

DIRECT SALES

Looking for Leads in All the Weird Places

Here are two ways to generate leads for new business:

- ❧ When a competitor files for bankruptcy, check the courthouse for documents on the case. Legal papers will list creditors and debtors—including companies that are looking for a new company to do business with.

- ❧ One CEO **telemarkets from his car phone**. When he passes a truck bearing the name and telephone number of a company that sounds like a possible customer, he dials the number on the spot, identifies himself, and asks to speak with the company's president. "I tell him I just passed his truck, and I'm calling in to report," says this CEO. "The guy usually laughs and asks how the driver is doing. You know, 'Did he hit you?'" Then the mobile salesman makes his pitch.

18
IDEA

DIRECT SALES

Encouraging On-Site Visits

The way Jim Ake figures it, "if we can convince a customer to visit our place, we'll make the sale about 90% of the time." Ake founded Electronic Liquid Fillers (ELF), a $15-million manufacturer, in LaPorte, Ind. The company encourages prospective buyers to make the visit by promising to **subtract the cost of a round-trip airfare from the first invoice** when they place an order.

At times, ELF gets a visit a day from prospective customers. To the 50% of ELF's customers that are small companies, the airfare offer can be the deciding factor on whether to fly out. Big-company customers, on the other hand, often don't even bother sending in receipts for reimbursement.

"When prospective customers see this company has meat on its bones and will be here to service the equipment, it means a lot," says Ake. "It's well worth the cost."

19
IDEA

DIRECT SALES

Integrate Your Direct Marketing

To compete successfully, you have to go beyond traditional marketing and sales efforts. Integrated direct marketing consultant and author Ernan Roman recommends that companies **combine their marketing efforts into a single package**. The costs, he contends, are not much higher, and the payoffs can be substantial.

Roman suggests, for instance, that every direct mail piece be combined with an 800 number in the package and a carefully timed follow-up phone call. The typical response rate for direct mail is 2%, but including an 800 number adds another 1% to 2% response, and making a phone call can tack on another 2% to 14%, according to Roman. By integrating just two marketing channels, direct mail and telemarketing, you may end up boosting your response rate to somewhere between 5% and 18%.

"The important issue is the aggregate response," says Roman, whose company, Ernan Roman Direct Marketing, is based in Queens, N.Y. "Does it make sense to let 98 people get stone cold while you're waiting for two responses to come in?"

Continuity Clubs for Everyone

There was a time when only book publishers persuaded customers to pay up front to receive a series of products in the mail by install-ment. Now companies in other consumer businesses are **applying the concept of continuity, or club, sales** to their own industries.

"When we didn't have much money, the club helped with cash flow," says Bruce Pavitt, cofounder of Sub Pop Records, the Seattle record label that launched Nirvana. To publicize the company early in its life, Pavitt produced limited editions of seven-inch singles and began a single-of-the-month club. Soon it had 2,500 members paying $35 or $60 in advance for 6 or 12 months of new music, giving the label a stronger national presence as well as upfront cash.

For Starbucks Coffee, the Seattle-based retailer and distributor of coffee, a coffee-of-the-month program meant a reduction in the cost of direct mail. "Instead of printing a catalog and getting just one order out of it, you get all these cumulative orders and can spread the marketing costs out over them," says Dwight McCabe, former mail-order director.

And club sales create a wonderful predictability of demand. When mail-order flower company Calyx & Corolla was starting out, flower-of-the-month-club sales accounted for at least 15% and as much as 40% of rev-enues, depending on the season. For the San Francisco company, that smoothed out fluctuations in what is a highly seasonal business.

21
IDEA

DIRECT SALES

Tap TV Shopping Channels

Mark Sneider's new products were definitely quirky—a Warm-up Scarf with a heating element and a bandanna with a cold pack attached called a "Cooldana." They weren't exactly flying off retailers' shelves, and Sneider's start-up company, Personal Comfort Corp., in Orlando, had no resources for print or television ad campaigns. If only, he figured, he could get onto one of the home-shopping networks, which live and breathe quirk. QVC, for example, has more than 50 million viewers who watch and buy products as they're being demonstrated on the air.

Sneider's first step was to **hook up with an agent who knows his way around the QVC network**. "You need a rep who is respected by QVC buyers and who isn't more than a few minutes from its headquarters," says Sneider. For a commission on sales, an agent can present your product to a buyer, usher it through quality control, track it into the warehouse, train the host, script the presentation, and decorate the set.

QVC was interested but required Personal Comfort to stock the network's warehouse with 5,000 units before airtime. The network also made Sneider agree to take back all unsold inventory. But by the end of the first 15-minute show, 2,500 units had found new homes. Sneider went on to appear nearly 100 times as a guest host, selling more than 250,000 scarves and bandannas through the channel.

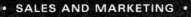

REAL WORLD

"These days growing my company feels like what happens when you play one of my kid's video games. You work like crazy to get to the next level, only to have the game become infinitely more complicated as a result."

JIM ANSARA
founder and CEO of Shawmut Design &
Construction, in Boston

22
IDEA

DIRECT SALES

Class Acts for Your Customers

I n certain industries, **customer education can generate immediate sales**. That's particularly the case for specialty retailers, who often have an untapped opportunity to teach customers about the products they sell.

Barnstable Grocery, a gourmet and specialty foods store, in Hyannis, Mass., put that theory into practice when it organized cooking classes. At first, the store offered free classes taught by local chefs and cooking instructors, attracting as many as 100 people per session. Later, then-owner Ron Cardoos taught the classes himself, charging $20 per session. He figures that although he was just breaking even on the fee, he was probably getting an additional $500 to $750 in sales after every class, since customers often bought the products he cooked with. Moreover, by teaching the classes himself, he had greater control over which products he showcased. He also established closer contact with customers. "It's selling," he says, "but it doesn't come across that way."

23
IDEA

The 60-Second Sales Pitch

Matt Hession realized that his target customers were much too busy to fit a standard sales call into their tight schedules. So he developed an irresistible solution: **a one-minute sales pitch**. When Hession takes off his watch to time himself, potential customers "think it's fascinating," he says. "They say to themselves, 'Hey, the entertainment just walked in.'"

Hession is president of Key Medical Supply, a $3.2-million company, in Thibodaux, La., and his customers are pharmacists, with whom he allies to sell or lease medical equipment such as wheelchairs. He needs "to be able to ride down the highway and make 15 to 20 cold calls a day. I can't have people say, 'Leave your card, and I'll call you back.'"

Using a carefully honed script, Hession tells pharmacists that he offers them a program just for independently owned drugstores that costs nothing and takes up little time. After 60 seconds, "I tell them my minute is up, because I want them to know that I am a person who means what he says. They are impressed that I manage to pull it off." When he calls a week later, he says, "This is Matt. I did the one-minute presentation. Have you had a chance to read over the contract I left with you?" Everyone remembers him. Even more impressive, he says 90% end up signing contracts.

24
IDEA

• SALES AND MARKETING •

GOING GLOBAL

Defending International Patents

There are no cheap ways to defend international patents. But once you've staked a claim in a country, it can pay to sue for small infringements every so often; a small suit can serve as a deterrent to other potential violators. "If you don't take an aggressive stand, the patent, in some cases, can be deemed ineffective," says Ross Mitchell, president of Acclimator Time, in Newton, Mass., which manufactures a jet-lag watch.

But lawsuits are lengthy, expensive, and stressful. Litigation should be far down on your list of intellectual-property priorities. One first step is to write a nonthreatening but firm letter to violators emphasizing your sole right to sell your invention or service in that country or bloc. Mitchell, for instance, has even **asked violators if they want to become licensees**. If the first letter is ignored, write a cease-and-desist order, with the help of a lawyer native to the perpetrator's country. Your general liability insurance may help cover legal fees.

25
IDEA

GOING GLOBAL

Software That Cuts Legal Fees

When Munchkin, a $15-million designer and marketer of baby bottles and other products for infants, needed a second international-distribution agreement, chief financial officer Betty Kayton didn't like either of her two choices. She'd either have to pay dearly to have a lawyer draw up a contract that would be almost identical to the first, or go it alone using the first contract as a template.

Munchkin's law firm, Boston-based Hale and Dorr, offered an appealing compromise: **interactive software for the company to draw up its own customized document**. The software prompted Kayton through a series of questions about her potential distribution agreement, flagging discrepancies such as how long she wanted the contract in place (longer than that particular country allowed) and clauses that would put the company at a disadvantage.

The lawyers then output the document, reviewed it, and drew up a legal memo on the foreign laws that could affect it. An international-distribution agreement typically costs between $3,000 and $5,000, but with the software, which the Van Nuys, Calif., company got for free from its law firm, the cost was only $1,500 the second time around.

GOING GLOBAL

From Easy Orders to Disorder

I t's not impossible for even the smallest companies to find, through trade shows, distributors willing to help sell in foreign markets. But if a deal sounds too good to be true, it could be.

Scott Montgomery, marketing chief at Cannondale, a bicycle manufacturer, in Georgetown, Conn., reports that back in 1989 when he started Cannondale Europe, distribution control became his biggest problem. Sales reached $1.5 million the first year, but margins slipped. The same distributors who placed large orders and paid with letters of credit began resorting to discounting. "When your products are being dumped," says Montgomery, "you lose control of pricing and positioning." In 1992, to reestablish his authority, he took the costly step of buying out the contracts of his European distributors and agents, for an "embarrassingly expensive" price of about 5% of the reps' annual commissions.

What he would have done differently, he now says, is **sign only a short-term agreement**. "You can do OK with agents and distributors if you protect yourself," he says. And he has: Cannondale Europe's annual sales are now about $32 million.

27
IDEA

Join the Club

Think you're too young to sell overseas? You're probably not. Many fast-growing small companies are going global. A poll of companies on the 1993 *Inc.* 500 list showed **38% doing business internationally**, averaging 15% of sales from abroad. The Commerce Department seconds the finding with even more compelling numbers: "very small" companies—those with fewer than 20 employees—accounted for 12% of U.S. exports as far back as 1987.

Number of *Inc.* 500 exporters doing business in...

Canada	84
Asia	73
United Kingdom	59
Japan	51
Germany	41
Mexico	39
Australia	30
South America	25
France	27
Italy	15
Spain	9

28
IDEA

GOING GLOBAL

Cooking Up Sales

When you're selling to a foreign prospect, the pomp and circumstance of formal meetings may actually get in the way of closing a deal. After years of selling internationally, Wayne Cooper decided to balance the formality with an evening of decidedly casual entertaining.

It began when Cooper, CEO of Arcon Manufacturing, in Charlotte, N.C., invited a delegation from China to his ranch to cook up their own favorite dishes. "They had been on the road for a month and missed their native cuisine," explains Cooper. Since then, Cooper has **turned his kitchen over to visiting business travelers** as often as once a month. Usually, the groups cook just for themselves, Cooper, and his wife, Judy.

The emphasis is on socializing, but, of course, there's often a business payoff in the end. In the case of the Chinese delegation, Arcon, which builds grain silos, closed a sale the very next day that it had been negotiating for a year and a half.

29

IDEA

• SALES AND MARKETING •

Combining Business and Pleasure

I f you think it's time to take your business overseas and if you're feeling burned out, consider letting one situation alleviate the other. That's what Dick Rubin did: when he decided to take Boston Metal Products global in 1990, he and his wife did it themselves—by moving to the Netherlands.

"I could have delegated the job to someone else," says Rubin, "but what would I be delegating? I didn't know anything about doing business in Europe. All I knew was that we belonged there, that there was a market for our products."

Three years after the move, international sales accounted for about 20% of the Medford, Mass., company's $20-million revenues and an equal percentage of its profits. Along the way, Rubin made a discovery about what he calls **"the power of the presidency."** "Everywhere I go, I run into middle managers of U.S. companies. I've yet to meet an American CEO. Evidently, people just don't realize the respect accorded presidents in Europe. It opens doors; it instills confidence that promises will be kept."

Rubin made a discovery about himself, too. "I took over my father's business in 1967. Today I feel as if my personal clock has gone back 25 years; I'm building something from scratch again, and I'm thriving on it. I feel revitalized."

30
IDEA

GOING GLOBAL

First Steps to Foreign Markets

Scouting out foreign markets can be intimidating. Where do you start when you've never tried it before?

There are **three steps a company can take to find overseas agents**. First, ask other businesses in your industry for the names of their distributors. Second, scan trade magazines that list overseas agents. And third, work through government agencies.

When ADM Technology, a manufacturer of media production equipment, in Troy, Mich., decided to set up an exporting network of agents, then-vice-president Murray Shields approached the U.S. Department of Commerce, in Detroit. He submitted a description of the kind of agent he needed and was given a list of names collected by Commerce officials through consulates and embassies overseas. Then he requested World Trade Data Reports on each agent, which gave him information on the candidate's customers, bank references, estimated sales volume, and assets. He narrowed his list to three agents per country and visited the candidates in person, checking in with each agent's customers while he was there.

Within a year, overseas sales were bringing in 30% of the company's then-$5 million in sales. The key is keeping in touch, Shields says. "You must be seen continuously by these people to say, 'Remember us?' They may not have sold anything for you since you saw them last, but you want them to keep trying."

31
IDEA

Faxable International Sales-Rep Form

Finding the right international distributors is one of the most diffi-cult—and crucial—steps in moving into the global marketplace. It's critical to assess how involved and productive a potential rep will be. One surprisingly simple move can help weed out at least half of the bad candi-dates: **send potential reps a one-page fax-back application**.

Electronic Liquid Fillers (ELF), in La Porte, Ind., started using the form in 1990. Foreign reps learn about the company at trade shows or from advertisements in trade magazines. They usually take the first step, phon-ing or faxing requests to represent the company. ELF then overnights packets of company information, including equipment spec sheets, press clips, and the application form. Nearly 50% of the reps bow out with-out responding. The form, says former vice-president of sales and mar-keting Jeff Ake, "dictates seriousness."

ELF receives about 18 inquiries a month from reps, many of whom have job assignments already in mind. The company screens out peo-ple working for direct competitors and looks for small companies that will give ELF focused attention. Registered reps are granted one-year account exclusivity for their prospective clients and leads. "We have international tigers actively promoting our equipment," says Ake.

In 1990, international business made up less than 15% of ELF's sales; by 1994, it had risen to 45% of the company's $15-million revenues.

• SALES AND MARKETING •

GOING GLOBAL

Exclusivity vs. Temporary Monopoly

L ining up good stateside distributors is challenge enough, but finding committed distributors overseas is even more daunting. Most foreign distributors want exclusivity. Should you grant it?

No—and yes. When PC Globe, a Tempe, Ariz., company that put the atlas onto software, first went overseas, managers cut deals with distributors offering exclusivity without any performance clause or insistence on a front-end order. Overseas product sales languished.

The company then changed its strategy. If distributors want exclusivity, PC Globe makes them order 20% of what they think they can sell in a year as their first order, which has to be prepaid. As long as distributors keep ordering the same amount each quarter, they retain their monopolies. **They don't get exclusivity as much as the *opportunity* for exclusivity**, say company execs, who add that the second strategy has worked out better for everyone.

33
IDEA

Packing for Foreign Trade Shows

I 've seen Americans at overseas trade shows who can't find their products, who've lost their equipment, and whose people were held up at customs," says Keith Kiel, vice-president of MacAcademy, a videotape distributor in Ormond Beach, Fla. He gives this advice on **what to bring (and what to leave at home)**:

- Copies of all documents. Kiel brings every fax he's received from the trade-show organizer. The paperwork can help smooth over situations where, for instance, you were promised audiovisual equipment and it's not there.

- A carnet. This detailed customs document listing all the valuables you take out of the States isn't required, but it can save you paperwork coming and going, and reduce the risk of being taxed on your own watch or luggage when you leave other countries.

- Half as much product and twice as many brochures as you think you'll need. Overseas customers, in Kiel's experience, respond better to a soft sell. They want a nice brochure to take home and study, which means fewer products sold at the show but more phone calls afterward.

- No equipment. Kiel rents everything, including computers and overhead projectors. He contacts manufacturers for the names of foreign distributors who can rent the equipment he knows he'll need. If there's no rental option, he always ships via the trade show's recommended carrier, even if it's more expensive than other carriers, because the recommended carrier usually can better help usher equipment through customs.

IDEA

INTERNET

Flameproof Online Marketing

Visions of a world of customers waiting behind the keyboard tempt many small businesses to try online marketing. But logging on to send direct-mail messages or ad copy to online forums such as newsgroups won't impress anybody. In fact, you're more likely to draw hate mail.

There are, however, subtle ways to **reach prospects through message boards**. Russian Information Services (RIS), a $1-million publisher and distributor of books about traveling in Russia, in Montpelier, Vt., has made a science of one approach. When RIS founder Paul Richardson started cruising the Internet, he made the mistake of posting a list of his books and their prices. The message was pulled by the system operator because it was too

much of an ad. After spending some time online and getting a feel for how the Internet really works, Richardson began responding to posted queries in the travel and international trade forums of online services. Now, when the person who posts a message requests information about Russian travel, Richardson answers questions and gives advice about everything from food to hotels to safety. At the end of his message, he suggests one of his books that might be of help. His postings close with a "business card": his name, company name, city, and state.

35

IDEA

<u>INTERNET</u>

Catch Customers on the Web

By early 1995, more than 1,800 companies were selling on the World Wide Web, one of the most commercially innovative parts of the Internet. Like their counterparts on online services such as CompuServe's Electronic Mall, Prodigy, and America Online, they target the millions of people who regularly scroll through the system.

Bill Murphy's wine company, Clos LaChance Wines, in Saratoga, Calif., was two years old, with $400,000 in annual sales, when he went onto the Web. For a screen-sized home page that includes the company's logo, its phone and fax numbers, an E-mail address, and a product description, Clos LaChance pays $50 a month to an Internet provider. A friend designed the page for Murphy; software to help put together a page would have cost about $150.

"We're a little bitty guy," says Murphy. "We cannot compete from an advertising standpoint with [much bigger wineries like Robert] Mondavi," but **on the Web, "our information will be as accessible as theirs."** And at such a low cost, the investment is incentive to learn how to navigate the online world.

36
IDEA

INTERNET

What's in an Internet Name?

I f you ever plan to do business on the Internet, **don't delay registering your business name as an Internet "domain name."** Richard Shaffer, owner of newsletter publisher Technologic Partners, in New York, learned that the hard way when he discovered that his choice, "technologic.com," was already taken by a company with a similar name.

How do you register? About 90% of new Internet users register their domain names through their Internet service providers, says Scott Williamson of Network Solutions, in Herndon, Va. Historically, anyone has been able to claim any untaken name, although that's changing. One reason is the case of Princeton Review, an *Inc.* 500 company. Princeton Review registered not only the name "review.com" but also the name "kaplan.com," after its arch rival, Kaplan Educational Centers. The people at Kaplan weren't amused. In a 1994 ruling suggesting that trademark law applied to Internet names, an arbitration panel ordered Princeton Review (which had sunk $30,000 into legal fees) to give up the "kaplan.com" handle.

MARKET RESEARCH

Using Customers as Beta Sites

The best way to test your product is to share it early and often with potential end users. That's what the software company Intuit, in Menlo Park, Calif., has done, and it's given the company domination of the market.

Intuit makes Quicken, the check-writing and financial-record software. In 1994, the company had revenues of $223 million. But back in 1984, when Intuit founder Scott Cook was starting out, all he knew from telephone research was that people would buy check-writing software only if it were faster and easier to use than a pencil. To test a prototype, he and the company's chief programmer, Tom Proulx, brought together a group of Junior League members. They did fine filling out the check outlines on their computer screens, but when it came time to print, they fumbled; the checks printed too high or too low. Cook and Proulx cringed. "We knew one thing," recalls Proulx, now retired. "If people had that much trouble the first time they used the program, they'd never use it again."

The company fixed the problem and continues to test relentlessly. One testing method, called "Follow-Me-Home," has Intuit **representatives observe new users** when they first use the product. "You watch their eyebrows, where they hesitate, where they have a quizzical look," says Cook. "Every glitch, every momentary hesitation is our fault." The testing helps the company figure out which areas to work on each time it updates its product.

38
IDEA

MARKET RESEARCH

Quick Reaction

I t might not be polished, but fast, informal feedback from potential customers is better than no feedback at all—especially when you're considering launching a new product and want to see whether there's any market for it at all.

When Randy Amon and a friend were first deciding whether to quit their jobs and start a business, they implemented what they recall fondly as **"the market-research minute"**: they called up one computer store. "We asked them, 'If we made a cable that connected opposing equipment, would you buy it?'" Amon remembers. "Not only did they say they'd buy it, they placed an order with us on the phone. We didn't even have a company yet, or a product." The store said it would pay $35 apiece for five cables, so the budding entrepreneurs went out with $100 and bought the materials to make them.

The market research even mutated into training: "The customer showed me how to make the cable," says Amon. That launched ABL Electronics, now of Hunt Valley, Md. Today it's a $10-million manufacturer of computer cables and a veteran on the *Inc.* 500.

REAL
WORLD

"Capitalism is faith in
the future. Talk about
faith. [My father] had
a one-truck
company called the
California Delivery
Service."

JACK KEMP
former Congressman
and U.S. Secretary of Housing and Urban
Development

39
IDEA

MARKET RESEARCH

When Staffers Do Research

When CEO Emma Lou Brent started a monthly contest for the best employee ideas at Phelps County Bank, in Rolla, Mo., it was more than just another suggestion program. Because employees are co-owners in the company through an employee stock ownership plan, they're well versed in the financials of the business. As a result, **the ideas they suggest are grounded in real life**—and are often the fruits of months or even years of market research.

For example, a customer-service rep might propose a marketing program aimed at senior citizens. That's what Phelps's Patti Douglas did, but only after she had spent nearly two years researching her idea. She dug up demographic statistics. She checked what every other financial institution in the area offered seniors. She tracked the bank's experience with its existing elderly customers. She costed out her proposal.

Today, Douglas's program has 325 customers over age 55, who belong to a club that gives them a special bank account and a variety of social activities. "It's a big success," says Brent.

40
IDEA

Focused Focus Groups

Focus groups are a good way to obtain customer feedback and plan for new products, according to Specialized Bicycle Components, of Morgan Hill, Calif. The company, which was founded in 1974 and has revenues of more than $160 million, conducts about 10 focus groups a year and believes they are key to its success. Kaylie Pirie, director of market research, says there are several things a company can do to get the most out of each session.

"Ask a friend to play moderator," Pirie says. "It's hard for a CEO to ask neutral questions, especially when he or she is the advocate of an idea." It's important to tell participants up front that there are no right or wrong answers, that you're not there to form a consensus, and that they should speak up when they don't like something. It also helps to start with easy questions, so that everyone feels comfortable speaking—questions, in Specialized's case, like "What brand of bike do you ride?" and "How many miles a week do you ride?"

"Good questions are usually open-ended, such as 'How did you go about selecting your last bike?'" says Pirie. "They force people to expand on their answers." And be sure to ask general questions—such as "What would your ideal bike be like?"—*before* you start asking about details. If you show participants a product right at the beginning, they end up spending the session concentrating mostly on that.

41
IDEA

MARKET RESEARCH

Focusing on Your Real Customers

Every now and then it pays to stop what you're doing and make sure you're really reading your customers right. You could be making presumptions that are costing you profits.

Mac McConnell, for instance, had always competed on price, assuming that was what mattered most to the customers of his Artful Framer Gallery, in Plantation, Fla. Then he **conducted a customer poll**, asking people who walked into the store over a six-week period to fill out a one-page survey about themselves, where they'd heard about the business, and how they rated the store's custom framing.

The 300 responses he gathered were full of surprises. Price was the lowest priority for customers; quality was highest, followed by uniqueness. That information gave McConnell the incentive to make some big changes: he dumped the low end of his product line and made museum-quality framing the standard. He began training his salespeople to take a consultative approach, first asking where the customer planned to hang the art and only then talking price. Because it turned out that word-of-mouth brought in one-third of the business, he started calling customers a month after their purchases to see if they were satisfied.

A year after the changes, the store's average invoice had risen from $67 to $167. Four years later, sales had tripled, and net profits were up 26%.

• SALES AND MARKETING •

MARKET RESEARCH

Capitalize on Disgruntled Customers

Some of the best sources of inexpensive, on-target market research are people who give your product a free trial and then turn it down.

Disappointed customers provide invaluable feedback for New Pig, a $30-million Tipton, Pa., manufacturer of bean-bag-like absorbents called "pigs" that soak up leaks around manufacturing machinery. The company's products are sent out with a 20-day, no-risk guarantee; if customers don't like them, they can ignore the bill. But when a bill is ignored, the company calls.

The upshot has been customer-suggested new or improved products. One customer, for instance, said he wasn't paying because the pig reacted badly with the nictric-acid leaks it was absorbing. At that point, New Pig didn't have a product to deal with hazardous fluids, and the comment inspired the company to develop one. Today, the hazardous-materials pig is a multi-million-dollar-a-year product.

The key to the strategy, says New Pig founder Donald Beaver, is the ignore-the-bill offer. Without it, dissatisfied customers would pay the first time but never order again, and the company would lose the opportunity to hear their immediate reactions.

43
IDEA

MARKET RESEARCH

Down-and-Dirty Forecasting

A lot of people have their own ways of informally gauging the health of the economy. One CEO, for example, keeps an eye out for how many stray golf balls he sees on a course. He figures, the more golf balls left behind, the more flush—and confident about the future—people are feeling. It's highly unscientific, but it makes an important point: there are all sorts of **indicators that divine the health of an industry or geographic area**.

Russell Inserra, for instance, has his own method for scoping out an area: before he takes any job he studies the regional price of bulldozers. The CEO of $26-million Triton Marine Construction, in Houston, has been tracking the regional auction prices of heavy equipment since he started the company in 1987 and has missed his share of economic storms because of it.

He never bids on contracts, no matter how promising, without running his test on the location. What's more, to identify up-and-coming states, Inserra compares the prices of the same equipment across the country. Inserra has found that the higher the prices, the better the regional economy. His accuracy? He's been right about 80% of the time.

44

IDEA

MARKET RESEARCH

Share and Share Alike

C hances are, outside your selling territory companies like yours are just as hungry for marketplace information as you are. If they aren't your competition, why not share secrets? That's what Sheila West, CEO of ACI Consolidated, in Monroe, Mich., figured when she was just starting out. She'd bought an archery retail shop full of bows and arrows, but she was in the dark about what to do next.

"I didn't know who else to call, and I needed to know what to order for the upcoming season," says West. So she **called other store owners for advice.** At first, people were suspicious of her motives, and hang-ups were common. Then West began offering the phone number of a manufacturer who would vouch for her. She conducted short interviews with about 20 shop owners and got a handle on which products were hot sellers, the best quality, and good prospects for the upcoming season. As she gathered information, she'd share it back. West, whose ACI is now a $9-million distributorship that spun off from the original store, says that "people who warmed up to the idea found they wanted to know about these things just as much as I did."

MATERIALS

Cheap Showmanship

There's so much noise and commotion at trade shows that if your product is unknown or very technical, it can seem impossible for your company to stand out.

That should have been a problem for Baird, a $30-million manufacturer of instruments that perform chemical analyses on metals—not exactly sexy stuff. But David March, director of sales and marketing at the Bedford, Mass., company, figured all he needed was a little creativity—and not even very much cash—to make an eye-catching display.

Before attending a show to introduce Baird and a new technology to a new market, March and his team searched customer files and found clients who had used the company's equipment to test cosmetics, jewelry, and children's toys. The company then ordered **huge props for the show**: giant toothpaste tubes, jumbo watches, and enormous crayons. "People would walk down the aisle, see these huge crayons, and come in to ask, 'What do you people do?'" reports March. He estimates that for a cost of $325 for prop rental, his booth's traffic was up 400%.

46

IDEA

MATERIALS

Easy Order Taking

When your staff is small, there's no reason not to make it easy for everyone to take customer calls and fill out an order form. That way, if your salespeople are out or busy, a customer won't slip through the cracks. When Gus Blythe, president of SecondWind, a Paso Robles, Calif., retailer of athletic-shoe-care products, first started, his goal was to **turn every employee into a potential order taker**.

His simple step: Blythe hung order forms from each desk at the company. That way, he says, when the phone rings, there is no excuse not to take an order. The forms are self-explanatory, and every employee is capable of filling them out. "There's nothing worse than making a customer wait to give you money," says Blythe.

47
IDEA

The Winning Ticket

With all the mail inundating your potential customers, it can be a challenge just to get your mail opened. One way to increase your odds: **stuff a lottery ticket into your package**.

Andy Juster and Scott Pilato, cofounders of Sunny Waterbeds, in Orlando, Fla., figured they could piggyback on the high profile of their state lottery. They put tickets into mailings that went out to their top 100 retailers, with the phrase "Lottery ticket enclosed" printed on the envelope. The mailing announced a new line of bedroom furniture and promised a follow-up call—both to pitch the product and to announce the winning number.

The result? When the company called a week later, 70% of prospects took the call and listened to the pitch. In the past, only 15% would take the call, adds Juster. "We were surprised" at how high the number was, he says. "You wouldn't expect people to hold onto a $1 lottery ticket for a week."

48
IDEA

Customer-Friendly Brochures

Face it: a lot of industrial marketing material is drop-dead dull. But it needn't be. If a company that manages hazardous waste can make what it does look appealing, there's hope for every marketer.

Geoffrey Swett, marketing director of Remediation Technologies (ReTec) in Tucson, wanted decent photos of refineries and hazardous-waste dumps for a new company brochure. So he and his ad agency turned to **stock-photography collections**, where handsome, albeit recycled, photos can be had on the cheap. Photo agencies specialize in everything from boardrooms to high tech, and their images can be rented for less money, almost always, than hiring a photographer.

Stock photos allowed ReTec to create customized marketing material for eight different niches. The same eight slides were used in each brochure. The slide depicting the industry highlighted was printed in color, while the rest were run in black and white. ReTec's total cost was about $2,300. A rough barometer: one-time rental of an image for the cover of an 8 ½-by-11-inch brochure with a print run of 10,000 generally costs between $600 and $1,000.

49

IDEA

MATERIALS

Put Prospects in the Picture

When customers are ruminating on a big-ticket purchase, you can make the decision a little easier by giving them a **Polaroid snapshot of the product they're considering**. That's what Domain home-furnishing stores do. Salespeople for the company, which is based in Norwood, Mass., and has 16 stores, provide photos and write their names and the product names on the back. The photos help customers feel more comfortable choosing Domain's furniture, explains founder and CEO Judy George, because they can compare it with products at other stores and with their own home furnishings.

Customers are also more inclined to keep the snapshot—and thus the salesperson's name and the product name—than a business card. "It helps them feel secure with the purchase and bonds them with the salesperson," says George. Bottom line: the low-cost practice increased Domain's sales-closing rate by about 25%.

IDEA

MATERIALS

Making It Easy to Be Found

Effective distribution is tough for any new consumer-product company. So when Elizabeth Andrews, CEO of Babybag of Maine, in Cumberland Center, Maine, began selling her infant outerwear, she **made sure buyers could find her even if they couldn't find a store that carried her goods**: she stitched the new company's address and phone number right on every clothing label.

When potential customers saw the products on babies at the grocery store or in the park, they could get the company phone number directly off the tyke. When customers called, they could place orders over the phone or find out the nearest store that carried the products.

"Later, when Babybag became better known, retailers objected to the phone number because they thought it would take business away from them," says Andrews. So now that distribution is broader, each piece of clothing carries just the company's address. But that's enough information for determined customers. "We still get plenty of calls from customers in rural regions who are serious enough about wanting our clothing that they dial information to get the number," says Andrews.

MOTIVATING SALESPEOPLE

Turn Salespeople into Profit Watchers

Manco, a fast-growing distributor of duct tape and other consumer products based in Westlake, Ohio, sells to Wal-Mart and other big customers. In the past, its salespeople—like most salespeople—competed for top-line revenues. Profitability was somebody else's worry.

Then the company began producing and distributing monthly account books that broke the company's numbers down by every conceivable category—including profits generated by each salesperson's accounts. At the same time, **the sales-compensation system was changed to take profitability into account**. As a result, salespeople began thinking of ways to improve the bottom line as well as the top.

"Now the sales guys ask me things like why their freight expense is up," says Charlie MacMillan, the company controller. "And I'll say, 'Well, let's take a look at your freight bill. Hey—you're shipping minimum-poundage loads to the West Coast! It's going to cost more money than if you're shipping a whole truckload.' So they'll say, 'We've got to get more on the order.'" In one year, a West Coast salesman cut his freight bill by 14%.

To Tom Corbo, Manco's president, sharing that information is a no-brainer. "People make better decisions once they know what they're being charged for."

52
IDEA

• SALES AND MARKETING •

MOTIVATING SALESPEOPLE

When You Sell into New Markets

I f your company develops a product line for a new retail market, **bring on new sales reps who know that industry cold**. That's what Koss Corp., a $36-million stereo-headphone maker, in Milwaukee, did when it started producing computer headphones and speakers in 1991, more than 30 years after the company was founded.

The company's longtime reps excelled at selling to stereo shops, but few had experience with computer stores. Rather than retrain them, sales vice-president John Koss split the line and hired six computer-rep firms to take on the PC headphones and speakers in several key markets. "There was this whole other world of reps I didn't know about," he says. "You love the ones who have buyers' home phone numbers." Recruiting market-savvy reps to nurture an unpredictable new product line paid off: between 1991 and 1994, sales of computer accessories grew to 25% of Koss Corp.'s total revenues.

53
IDEA

MOTIVATING SALESPEOPLE

Make Prospecting Pay

One problem with paying salespeople fixed-rate commissions is that, with enough steady customers, they can get lazy. Content to service the customers they know, they may be less eager to sniff out prospects. Bill Bozeman, CEO of Delta Audio-Visual Security, in New Orleans, found that **paying an extra 1% commission for first-time customers** solved the problem for him.

Salespeople at the alarm-system company normally earn between 4% and 12% commission. On a $50,000 installation, the extra 1% is another $500. It may not sound like a lot, but the opportunity to earn a bit more has influenced how Delta salespeople—especially the younger ones—spend their time. In the first two years of using the incentive, new-customer sales rose from 25% of revenues to more than 35%. "Once we have them," Bozeman says, "we're in a strong position to convert them to regular customers."

54
IDEA

You Earn It, You Keep It

Here's a great way to motivate salespeople: give them a new technology toy, but tell them they can keep it only if they produce.

That's what Pat Kelly, CEO of Physician Sales & Service (PSS), in Jacksonville, Fla., did with his medical-instruments salespeople. He wanted them to sell a load of examination tables within 60 days, so he **gave them the sales incentive up front**: cellular phones they could keep if, as a team, they sold enough. "Once they got used to the phones, I knew they wouldn't want to turn them back in," says Kelly, who had the phones installed while he was offering his sales force the challenge at a meeting.

Each of the 12 sales offices had to sell one $4,000 table for each salesperson in the office. If an office fell one table short, its salespeople would have to chip in and buy one phone. But the incentive did the trick: the sales force not only reached its goal of 70 tables but surpassed it, selling 105—with no returns.

55
IDEA

PARTNERING

Making Your Customer Your Partner

Even if you've developed a wonderful retail product and garnered great results from focus groups and test markets, you still have to get through the toughest hoop: selling your product to the buyers for the nation's retailers. If they're not convinced that your product will work in their stores, then your product will never reach their shelves. Norman Melnick, chairman of Pentech International, a $62-million maker of pens and markers, in Edison, N.J., makes sure that his products get on shelves by **bringing buyers in on packaging decisions**.

Before going into production, Pentech lets buyers shape the final product. Do they want pens in 16-packs instead of 8-packs? Fine. They think the package takes up too much space on the shelf? No problem; the packaging will shrink.

By becoming part of the manufacturing and marketing process, buyers develop a vested interest in the product's success, reports Melnick. There's one catch: Pentech asks that in return for its accommodating buyers, the buyers place a formal purchase order before Pentech starts production.

56
IDEA

• SALES AND MARKETING •

<u>PARTNERING</u>

Know Thy Partner

I f you're thinking about approaching a large company to become a strategic partner with your smaller business, you need to answer two key questions: What are the needs of that company, and will that company believe you can help it?

When Ruth Owades got the idea in 1987 to start Calyx & Corolla, a mail-order flower catalog based in San Francisco, she knew she'd need big partners—growers to provide the product and Federal Express to deliver it. So she **researched both industries to make sure she understood their pressures**. To growers, she'd offer sporadically heavy but consistent business. "We get them orders the day *after* Valentine's Day," she says. For the shipping industry, she focused on the increased competition wrought by fax machines. "When I was in business school I studied the Federal Express start-up case. I knew carriers like FedEx were having to change their mind-set; they had filled their planes with lovely flat envelopes and now had to adapt to the challenges of moving boxes."

Owades was confident that she was being realistic about her goals. She had founded the successful catalog Gardener's Eden, which she thinks made the difference: "I don't think you could attempt a project of this magnitude without that kind of credibility." Still, it took about three months of negotiation to get her relationships in place.

57
IDEA

PARTNERING

Tie in with Big Brands

Leslie Lawrence and Nancy Urbschat run a small ad agency and got into the new-products business when Lawrence became pregnant. "I wanted to keep a journal during my pregnancy," she says, but not finding anything she liked, the partners created a 40-week undated calendar they christened "Mother in the Making."

The duo decided that the product "wouldn't do well sitting in a bookstore." Instead, they figured they'd try to **get a big company to help them market it as a product tie-in**. Their target: Warner-Lambert, maker of e.p.t., a home-pregnancy test. Their goal was to get a calendar offer tucked into each e.p.t. box. But first they had to get a meeting with e.p.t.'s product manager, and that took a good six months.

When Lawrence and Urbschat showed up, they were prepared. They arrived at the meeting with a marketing strategy in hand, which distinguished their idea from the other pregnancy-related product ideas the manager had seen. Five months later, they had a contract: the East Longmeadow, Mass., entrepreneurs and their company, The Super Market, would print the coupons and calendars at their own expense, and Warner-Lambert would receive $1 per sale. A year later, the offer hit the shelves. Orders were sluggish, but the exposure was worth it: a vitamin company and a hospital called, both requesting deals to use the calendars as premiums.

58

IDEA

• SALES AND MARKETING •

PRICING

Pricing Pitfalls

I t's common to cut special deals for big customers, but be careful: the courts are again looking at whether the practice is illegal. A recent case spotlights the thorny issue. The American Booksellers Association (ABA), acting on behalf of small independent booksellers, filed suit in 1994 against five publishers, charging them with unjustly giving big chains better prices and promotional allowances.

The ABA suit invokes the Robinson-Patman Act, a 1936 antitrust statute that **prohibits companies from discriminating among customers by offering special terms** that can't be justified by costs or competition. "For better or worse, Robinson-Patman is having a rebirth," says lawyer James Calder, a partner at Rosenman & Colin, in New York City. As a result, it could be illegal, warns Calder, to drop your price to some customers but not all. "Your competitor could have a case against you, or you might be sued by a customer who did not receive the volume discount."

The ABA suit is worth watching and having your lawyer follow up on.

59
IDEA

PRICING

Underpricing Is as Bad as Overpricing

You want customers to think they're getting a good deal, but there's no point in selling yourself short. If you underprice yourself, customers might think you're worth less, and you could lose profits for no reason. One way to determine the best price point: **conduct a direct-mail campaign that tests different offers**.

When Approach Software, in Redwood City, Calif., launched its first product in 1992, it wanted to offer a low introductory price to persuade users to try its database software program. Jaleh Bisharat, Approach's marketing director, interviewed prospects and got confirmation that the $149 she was considering was reasonable. Then, to be sure, she sent out 50,000 direct-mail offers with price points of $99, $129, and $149. The mailing provided the "statistical proof" Bisharat needed when sales came in almost as high at $149 as at $129. The company then tested a $199 price, but that "crossed a threshold of what people would spend to try a new product through the mail," says CEO Kevin Harvey.

The low initial price did its job. One month after the product began shipping, Approach 1.0 landed on industry best-seller lists. Three months later, the company raised the suggested retail price to $399 ($279 street price)—and the product has remained a top seller.

IDEA

Pricing by the Numbers

For a business that creates a custom product, good estimates make or break profits. Wall/Goldfinger, a Northfield, Vt., manufacturer of contract office furniture, estimated jobs in longhand for its first 20 years, but in 1990 it **computerized the estimation process**. Using off-the-shelf databases that cost less than $1,000, the $3-million company now can price and adjust jobs in a fraction of the time it once took.

The program allows general manager David Haber simply to type in a description of a job, the materials needed, and the number of hours the assignment should take. The computer then lists all the procedures needed to execute it, adds up the hours each step requires, multiplies the totals by the billing rates, adds a company markup, and voilà—a price is born.

Sales reps can negotiate faster with customers, because the company can adjust quotes within seconds when a salesperson calls from a customer's office with a question like, "What if we change the veneer to oak?" Bottom line: in the time since it's added the more efficient price-quote process, Wall/Goldfinger's business has tripled, and profits have stayed stable.

61
IDEA

PRICING

Sweetening the Deal

How do you make that first sale if your products are priced above the market? One trick is to **create a combined package** that's too good to pass up.

That was the strategy used by Al Burger, founder of "Bugs" Burger Bug Killers, a Miami-based exterminator company. The company's standard fee for pest elimination at restaurants was so out of line with the competition that many potential customers didn't give the company a second look. So the company came up with a second service. For an additional fee, its workers also clean refrigerator coils, reset seals, and otherwise help restaurants control their energy costs. In many cases, annual cash savings to the restaurant customer cover the cost of the pest service. The catch: customers can't get the energy service without signing up for pest control as well.

• SALES AND MARKETING •

PRICING

Avoid the Price-Cut Trap

Bundling products together can help move regularly priced products when sales go soft—especially when the market for the product is weak to begin with.

That's what Chuck Sussman found when he was running Pretty Neat Industries, in Pompano Beach, Fla., and sales of his cosmetics-organizer began to fall off. He didn't want to cut prices, because that probably wouldn't have generated enough new sales to make up for the loss in profitability per sales unit.

"I had already been planning to introduce a new version of the organizer at about half the regular price," recalls Sussman. "Instead, I priced the cheaper model at about 90%, shrink-wrapped the old and new products into one package, and stuck on a Day-Glo banner that said 'Free $4 Value with This Purchase!'"

Not only were Sussman's margins higher on the combination pack than they would have been if he'd sold the products separately, but the package sold like crazy. "Customers kept the expensive product and gave the inexpensive one as a gift," Sussman says. "And, of course, we wound up increasing our margins, not cutting them, which is what would have happened if we'd cut prices."

63
IDEA

PUBLIC RELATIONS

Letter Quality

Don't miss an easy opportunity to communicate what's important about your business with your correspondence. Run **a compelling tagline on your company's stationery**.

North American Tool & Die (NATD), a metal-stampings company in San Leandro, Calif., has an eye-catching statement at the bottom of its stationery: "0.1% Customer Rejects Since 1980." The company finds that the concrete detail about its quality has far greater impact than an abstract company slogan.

Customers surveyed by the $20-million business expressed incredulity at the low rejection rate. That's just fine with NATD execs, who decided that's all the more reason to keep the number in front of customer eyes.

• SALES AND MARKETING •

IDEA

Do-It-(Mostly)-Yourself PR

Barb Oakley couldn't afford a full-service public relations firm when her company, FireFly Flashcards, was a start-up in Utica, Mich. The company she'd approached said a six-month campaign would cost $19,000, which she didn't have. So Oakley proposed a different way of working. She asked the PR agency if it would **take her on as a client but charge just by the hour**. She figured she could use help in brainstorming ideas, editing press releases, and targeting publications, but that she could do the rest by herself.

The PR agency, Hermanoff & Associates, in Detroit, said yes. Oakley met with principal Sandy Hermanoff every two months to think up new angles. Oakley drafted the releases, Hermanoff edited them, and Oakley typed them up and mailed them out. The cost of the campaign—which got FireFly into local and national newspapers and magazines—was a more manageable $500 for Hermanoff's time and $250 for mailings and follow-up calls. "It gave us a far more professional effort at a reasonable cost," says Oakley.

65
IDEA

PUBLIC RELATIONS

Get Your Mug in the Newspaper

Some CEOs are too shy to play spokesperson. And then there's Pete Slosberg, founder of Pete's Brewing, in Palo Alto, Calif.

In 1994, Slosberg's publicity pro, Kristin Seuell, came up with the idea to celebrate one million cases sold and got Slosberg to pose for a newspaper publicity shot in a bathtub, surrounded by his liquid assets. But rather than just send the photo and a press release scattershot to newspapers, she filed the photo with PhotoWire, a commercial service of Business Wire, which **sends photos digitally into the darkrooms of more than 370 newspapers** as well as ABC and CNN. The caption: "Specialty brewers make it from bathtub to big time."

The color photo was picked up by 35 papers, including the *San Francisco Chronicle, Arizona Republic,* and *Orlando Sentinel.* The filing cost: $725, which was "worth every cent," says Seuell.

TECH
TIP

66
IDEA

PUBLIC RELATIONS

Write on the Money

You want visibility in your industry, but a full-page, four-color ad in a trade magazine can run into thousands of dollars. Ron Harper, chairman of Harper Companies International, a $17-million holding company, in Charlotte, N.C., figured out a way to get publicity without spending a lot of money.

Harper offered a **$500 bonus to any employee who could write a technical article and get it published** in a trade magazine. The first 10 people who met the challenge cost the company $5,000, but yielded what Harper estimates was $40,000 worth of promotion. "Plus," he says, "the articles have a lot more credibility than an ad." To boost editorial productivity, the company lined up a local freelance writer whom the employees could work with for a share of their $500. That took away some of the hesitation of people who wanted to try but were shy about their writing skills.

67
IDEA

PUBLIC RELATIONS

Picking a PR Firm

If you're thinking about hiring a public relations firm, don't forget to **check out its reputation with the reporters who cover your industry or region**. When it comes to assessing a firm's reputation as a publicist, "reporters know better than anyone if we're good at our job," says Sally Jackson, president of Jackson & Co., a Boston public relations firm. Reporters, after all, are on the receiving end of agency letters and calls. They know which firms they pay attention to and which they ignore. And they generally won't hesitate to tell you if the agency you're considering is one that they respect or one that makes them cringe. (On the other hand, reporters may not know which firms are best at crisis management or strategic planning, other services that qualified PR firms provide. You'll have to get that information from the firm's clients.)

There's another advantage to calling reporters for references: you will be introducing them to your company, which won't hurt your future public relations efforts. It's always beneficial to have your own direct contacts with the media.

II

"When I get an angry guest on the phone, screaming because—I tell you no lie—he doesn't like the kosher pickle we serve on the side with our sandwiches, I'm thinking, 'Get a life,' while I'm saying, 'What kind of pickle would you like?' Because the issue isn't the pickle with the strong hint of garlic. The issue is making the guy feel good.

"The customer is not always right. The customer knows it. You know it. Your employees know it. In fact, customers are frequently misinformed, unclear, and selfish. Who cares? It's not the issue. Make them feel good, and you'll be giving them what they really want: *satisfaction*."

JEFFREY MOUNT
president of Wright's Gourmet House,
a restaurant and catering company, in Tampa

68

IDEA

COLLECTIONS

Closing the Sale (Completely)

I s it a cynic or a realist who says that any company that's never had an accounts-receivable problem either isn't looking very hard or isn't selling very hard? Either way, most companies do admit to having bad debt. One way for a business to cut down on difficult collections is to **tie salespeople's commissions to the collection of receivables**.

The way managers at Macke Business Products, based in Rochester, N.Y., figure it, it all depends on how you define a sale. For 20 years, the office-products distributor has run under the theory that a sale doesn't count until the money comes in. As a result, a salesperson's commission is reduced by 5% if an account is 60 days past due; 10% at 90 days; and lost altogether at 120 days.

The assumption is that a call to a delinquent customer from the company's credit department is probably less effective and more alienating than a reminder from the salesperson in charge of the account. As for the sales force itself, the system encourages greater awareness of customers' financial stability. Salespeople go on every sales call with a binder that includes a weekly sales printout, inventory accounts, and the monthly aging reports on that particular account's payment history.

69
IDEA

COLLECTIONS

No Pay, No Work

When James Stroop was president of a $12-million construction company, he took a hard line when it came to getting paid. He would **stop work on any job for which payments were 20 days overdue**.

The company would bill for projects monthly, sending out invoices on the 25th of the month. Payment was due on the 5th or 10th day of the following month. By the 12th day, Stroop would get a list of customers whose payments hadn't been received, and on days 15 through 18, he and his account managers would begin hitting the phones, warning delinquent customers that projects would have to be shut down if payment wasn't received promptly. That usually did the trick. But if it didn't, construction would grind to a halt on day 25, to be resumed only after a cashier's check had been deposited in the company's coffers.

In 15 years, the company wrote off less than $5,000 of bad debt. Companies have lots of leverage, notes Stroop. All they have to do is be willing to use it.

70
IDEA

COLLECTIONS

Writing Off Temptation

Without becoming paranoid about your own employees and their relations with customers, it's still important to think about what protections you have in place to ensure that fraud isn't overly tempting. Many companies, for instance, have only the loosest procedures for handling bad-debt write-offs, which leaves them exposed to collusion between people in their accounting staffs and delinquent customers.

"Companies should set up formal mechanisms to **control the points at which debts are either turned over to collection agencies or written off**," advises Richard Rampell, CEO of Rampell & Rampell, an accounting firm, in West Palm Beach, Fla. Company CEOs or chief financial officers, he says, ought to be required to give signed approval before either action occurs.

Rampell also recommends that companies set up controls to make sure that all deposits on sales agree with the total payments of individual customers, as recorded in accounts-receivable balances. Careful organization, he says, is the best way to make sure that there have been no mistakes or theft.

COLLECTIONS

Postdate Headaches

Sooner or later you have to deal with them: new customers who are short on cash and haven't yet established a credit record with you. They may urge you to trust them when they say they'll pay in a few weeks. Or they may ask to pay with a postdated check.

Postdated checks are somewhat better than verbal promises and may be the only alternative. But if you decide to take the check, be sure to **consult a lawyer about the laws in your state regulating postdated checks** (yes, there may be such rules). Some states require that a few days before you cash the check, you must remind the customer in writing that you have it and that you are planning to cash it.

72
IDEA

COLLECTIONS

Collection No-No's

Don't even think about adopting an alias when pursuing credit deadbeats. It's illegal in some states. Even the most innocuous action can prove risky. If, for example, your company relies on an in-house lawyer to pursue creditors, it can wind up in hot water if your lawyer's stationery does not indicate that he or she is a company staffer. For a free brochure, *Twenty-Seven of the Most Dangerous Traps for Creditors and Collectors*, by Alan D. Reffkin, call Western Union Commercial Services (800-624-5472).

73
IDEA

Computer Gets Personal

For years, White Dog Cafe, in Philadelphia, printed out daily menus on its computer, but president Judy Wicks was never completely happy with them. "The typeset copy lacked a sense of immediacy. The psychology just wasn't right," says Wicks. Changing typefaces regularly didn't work; Wicks found that competitors quickly latched onto the latest fonts.

Her solution: **create a computer font of the handwriting of the restaurant's chef**, Wick's partner, Kevin von Klause. Once the font is loaded into a printer, a computer's keyboard becomes a pen, with a point width that can range from the bluntness of a felt-tipped marker to the fine line of a rapidograph.

"It's ironic," says Wicks. "When we first opened the restaurant, I handwrote the menus because we couldn't afford a computer. Now we're choosing to spend money on automation so we can look more homegrown." Wicks has also had a font made of her own handwriting for personal memos, bulletin-board postings, invitations to staff parties, and letters to customers. Her software program of choice: PenFont ($49.50 from Signature Software, Hood River, Ore.).

74
IDEA

COMMUNICATION

Passing Ideas to Customers

Good ideas have a way of slipping through the cracks if there's no method for collecting and distributing them. At Berthelot & Associates, a management-consulting and accounting firm, in Cleveland, employees are expected to be on the lookout for ways that clients can save money or increase income. So the company developed a simple form that accompanies each client's file. Called **the "pay-for-me" form**, it provides space—and serves as a reminder—for notes and suggestions about ways to save money.

"People were always coming up with ideas for clients but forgetting them in the press of business," says Mike Berthelot. "In busy periods, the form keeps the staff focused on doing what our clients hire us to do." The form also gets people who aren't normally considered customer-support people, like clerical workers, involved in helping clients.

And one other thing: clients love it. "When I tell prospective clients about the pay-for-me forms," says Berthelot, "they're thrilled."

75

IDEA

The Other Kind of Customer Credit

Customers can be a good source of new product ideas, but if you don't acknowledge their contributions you're missing out on a great chance to lock in their loyalty.

That's not a danger for a company in Cleveland, which goes so far as to **give plaques to customers who offer suggestions** that lead to new products. The company, Crescent Metal Products, manufactures and distributes equipment for the food-service industry.

When a food-service director of the San Diego schools approached Crescent with an idea for a mobile serving table for the school yard, Crescent took the suggestion and ran with it. The table the company developed became one of its top 25 products out of more than 800. In appreciation, president George E. Baggott presented the food-service director with a plaque and publicized her contribution in the company newsletter and the trade press. He's since done the same with other customers, which encourages others to pass on ideas. It wins the company a few points, too.

76
IDEA

COMMUNICATION

You Oughta Be in Pictures

Want to get a prospect's attention? When prospective customers visit Eriez Magnetics, a $50-million manufacturer of magnetic laboratory equipment and metal-detection equipment, the receptionist **lines them up under a sign with the company trademark and snaps their pictures.** "It's our way of saying that we're complimented you'd come all the way to Erie, Pa., just to see us," says Chet Giermak, CEO and president.

The photos have a practical purpose as well. Giermak sends them to the visitors along with a letter reminding them whom they met with and what they talked about. He slips the photo into a cardboard frame with the company's mission statement on the back. "It's a little memento," says Giermak. It also makes it easier for the company to take a second crack at making a sale if Eriez didn't get it the first time.

It takes only a minute to dictate the letter and costs only about $2 per package. "Most people like to have their picture taken," adds Giermak. "It makes them feel important."

77

IDEA

• CUSTOMER RELATIONS •

COMMUNICATION

Plugging Your Customers

O ne good way to reinforce your relationship with customers is to plug them whenever you can. At San Luis Sourdough, a $3-million bakery in San Luis Obispo, Calif., that means **running ads in the company newsletter promoting customers**.

Linda and Dave West, who own and manage the business, say they could have found paying advertisers for the quarterly six- to eight-page publication, which goes out to the company's 80 employees. Instead, they use the space to promote whatever their customers want and, of course, mention that those businesses carry the company's bread. "It's another way to thank the people who do business with us," says Dave West.

78
IDEA

COMMUNICATION

Contact at Every Job

Think twice before creating a system in which customers deal only with salespeople. Often you can provide better service—and run your company more efficiently—if you **let customers deal directly with the people who help make the product**.

It was with that thought in mind that Hugh Vestal reorganized his machine-tool business, Carbide Surface, in Clinton Township, Mich. Customers who need a tool coated with carbide talk directly with one of the five "impregnators" who actually do the coating. The impregnator schedules the job, arranges for delivery of the part, performs the work, and submits a job-cost form to Vestal, the president of the company.

Customers like the system because it spares them from having to work through intermediaries. Shop workers like it because it challenges them and breaks up the monotony of the job. And salespeople like it because it frees them to concentrate on getting new business.

79
IDEA

• CUSTOMER RELATIONS •

COMMUNICATION

Facts via Fax-Back

L ike many small-company founders, Stephen Siegel used to be part executive, part customer-service rep. His eight-employee company, UV Process Supply, in Chicago, sells mail-order technical supplies to companies that use ultraviolet light in printing. When customers had equipment problems, they'd call Siegel, who has worked in the industry for about 20 years. That was great for customers but not so great for Siegel, who often spent one-third of his day taking such calls.

What changed? Siegel invested in a **fax-on-demand program**. Now, customers with questions get connected to an automated system that allows them to choose from hundreds of documents that cover all kinds of technical queries. Documents chosen by a customer are automatically sent out by fax for free. The technology has been around since the late 1980s, but prices are just becoming more affordable for small companies; products are available for less than $1,000.

UV Process Supply has integrated the service into its catalog, with each product description now accompanied by instructions for obtaining additional information by fax. Siegel reports that the system averages 15 to 20 calls a day, and all but the most technophobic customers use it. He also estimates that the entire fax-on-demand program has reduced his time on the phone by about 85%.

REAL
WORLD

"It's not that new technology makes the current level of our performance easier to meet; it's that the bar has been raised, and our clients demand more from us. It's like a just-in-time delivery of ideas."

ALLAN ARLOW
former CEO of the Computer &
Communications Industry Association,
in Washington, D.C.

COMMUNICATION

Polling for Peanuts

Almost three out of four independent retailers see themselves as just poor to fair at gathering customer information, according to a survey by Arthur Andersen and the Illinois Retail Merchants Association. But there *are* cheap ways to tap customers.

Beth Willey, who with her father runs Henderson's Department Store, in Sycamore, Ill., **polled customers by sending a mail-in survey to 1,200 charge-card shoppers**. With no incentive other than goodwill, 592 sent back the three-page questionnaire within weeks, and more replies trickled in for months.

Designed with the help of two local marketing students, the survey included this open-ended question: If you owned Henderson's, what would you do to change it? "I was ready to hear it. We got comments on everything," says Willey. A lot of people signed their names to the survey, and Willey tapped them for the store's first-ever focus group.

81
IDEA

COMMUNICATION

The Personal Touch

Personal contact with customers is a crucial element in the success of any new business—and it's one of the most common casualties of growth. "As a company grows, the president tends to fade away into his office," observes Joseph Cherry, president of Cherry Tire Service, in Maybrook, N.Y. That can lead to a loss of leverage right at the point when a company is starting to take off and needs it most.

The danger is that the company can become just another faceless entity that a customer deals with every day. The danger is even greater, Cherry realized, in an era when companies rely on computers to handle communications with customers. So he instituted a simple policy of **sending a personal thank-you note to each customer**. Now, every evening he sits down and signs a stack of cards printed with "Thank you" on the front and, inside, a message reading, "Thank you very much for calling Cherry Tire Service. We really appreciate your business."

"It's hard to keep up with, but it's worth it," says Cherry. "It's better than newspaper ads because each card goes right to the person I want to reach. And customers don't forget it."

82

IDEA

Using Customer Databases Daily

One-to-one relationship selling is the oldest game around, but if you're not working it in conjunction with a well-maintained customer database, opportunities are slipping by.

Silverman's, a men's-apparel chain in North and South Dakota, has a close enough relationship with customers that its database is filled with up-to-date information about individual shoppers' sizes, buying habits, and preferences—even products they tried on and didn't buy. Salespeople use the information to help friends buy gifts and to follow up on big sales; a **self-generated computer report** two weeks after the sale reminds the salesperson to call and check that everything is satisfactory. "Most customers would rather stop shopping at a store than take the trouble to complain," says third-generation clothier Stephen M. Silverman.

The marketing department uses the database to target its efforts. It produces a simple postcard announcing the arrival of, for instance, bathrobes made by a prominent designer. The computer selects customers who have previously purchased the designer's merchandise and have not purchased bathrobes in the past year. Silverman says that such targeted mailings typically elicit a 25% response rate in four weeks for his business—and that's with no discount.

83
IDEA

COMMUNICATION

Tracking Customer Comments

Stonyfield Farm, a Londonderry, N.H., yogurt maker, had hoped its new apricot-mango flavor would take off, but the company wasn't prepared for the accolade it received from one customer: so taken was the woman with the new flavor's color that she brought a container down to the local hardware store and asked a clerk to mix up a batch of like-colored paint for her bedroom.

Stonyfield CEO and president Gary Hirshberg can share thousands of comments like that, because his company makes a point of soliciting and carefully tracking what customers think about its yogurt (and its yogurt's colors). With a note on the side of each of its containers asking for comments, the $20-million business gets about 150 calls and letters each week from customers.

The gist of **each message is entered into a database** that Hirshberg and other managers pore over for opportunities to cement customer loyalty, spot promising new niches, and fine-tune the product line. Large companies have been using sophisticated systems to analyze consumer feedback for a long time, but now more small and midsize companies are enlisting technology to press what should be an inherent advantage in personalized service and focused marketing. All it takes to get started is a customized database. You can create it in-house or hire a consultant. It should take somewhere between 12 hours and a couple of weeks to develop the system you need.

84
IDEA

COMMUNICATION

Opening Your Books to Customers

Few companies show their financial statements to their customers—they're afraid that if customers find out what their margins are, they will try to negotiate better prices. That may be the case, but it may also be true that if you're delivering value, it's at a price customers are prepared to pay—otherwise they wouldn't be your customers. And presumably, they have an interest in keeping their vendors happy.

There can be real value in being completely open with customers. That's why Manco, a fast-growing distributor of duct tape and other consumer products, based in Westlake, Ohio, **tracks its costs, customer by customer, and then shows the figures to them**. Each customer sees exactly what Manco makes on its business, which is exactly the point. Customers can see, for instance, that they aren't paying for somebody else's freight. That, says Tom Corbo, president of Manco, gives the company a competitive advantage.

85
IDEA

COMMUNICATION

Greeting the E-Mail Nation

Take a tip from companies on the cutting edge: before long, your customers will be demanding **electronic mail access to your business**.

For instance, Checkfree, a Columbus, Ohio, company that provides an electronic-bill-payment service, gets fully two-thirds of its customer-service queries by E-mail. That's changed the way the company has had to educate its employees: customer-service reps are trained in both phone and online mail etiquette. Checkfree has arranged for customers to have a direct E-mail connection without having to log on to a commercial service, and customers receive replies within 24 hours.

Meanwhile, Joe Boxer, a San Francisco clothing company, sells through retail buyers and the Internet, skipping catalogs altogether. The Internet is *the* way to reach younger fans, says marketing chief Denise Slattery. The company encourages E-mail by printing its online address on its clothing hangtags and on billboards. The messages that come over the wire range from the conversational "Yo dude, love your underwear" to the more pressing "What briefs should I wear on a first date?" But Joe Boxer may end up issuing a catalog yet: onliners keep bugging the company to do so.

TECH TIP

86
IDEA

Next-Day Relay

Keeping up with correspondence can be a colossal task. To make sure important letters are answered swiftly but carefully, Measurement Specialties has a **two-step system of first acknowledging and then answering all letters**.

Donald Weiss, CEO of the Fairfield, N.J., manufacturer of measurement devices, says that within 24 hours, a short note goes out to the party saying the letter was received and to expect further correspondence by a specified date—usually within a week. Next, the person in charge of the area that the letter concerns drafts a letter and lets it sit for a day before sending it around the office for others to read.

"Too many companies dash off a reply," says Weiss. "Our customers are prepped for a timely response. And we avoid shooting from the hip."

87
IDEA

COMPLAINTS

Capitalizing on Complaints

Common sense isn't that common, which is why simple things like **asking an angry customer what he or she would like you to do** can seem like such a remarkable tactic.

"First let the customer sound off," says John Wirth, president of Woodworker's Supply, a mail-order company, in Albuquerque. After the venting, ask how the situation can best be resolved. "Ninety percent of the time the customer comes back with something reasonable—often less than you would volunteer to do yourself," says Wirth. And Wirth doesn't leave these opportunities to chance: employees are trained to handle complaints in sessions with simulated calls.

The payoffs are huge. "A customer with a satisfactorily resolved problem will produce three times the revenue of a customer without a problem," contends Wirth. "Down the road, when you and six other competitors reach his mailbox, your mailing will stand out. The customer develops an affinity for you that he doesn't have for the others." And, he adds, the customer will probably recommend you to friends.

IDEA

Preempting Refund Requests

Sometimes even guaranteed service falls short. If you offer a guarantee and fail to meet it, your job, according to Walter Riley, is to turn that minus into a plus. Riley's company, G.O.D. (Guaranteed Overnight Delivery), doesn't just offer a money-back guarantee—**it sends customers their refunds before they ask for them**.

The Kearny, N.J., overnight express freight company sends monthly invoices to its customers' accounting departments, but it also has regular correspondence with customers' purchasing departments. Purchasing agents receive reports detailing the previous month's deliveries and, if any deliveries were missed, the refund check.

Dealing with the purchasers, not just the accounting department, is the key, says Riley, because "the people who pay the bills don't decide who to use. This kind of itemized report really impresses purchasers, who 99% of the time don't even know they should get money back." He adds that "a record and check are relatively simple for us to generate but would be a hassle for them. And they look better upstairs."

The policy not only provides G.O.D.'s salespeople with more to offer but also keeps the company's performance statistics rigorously up to date.

89
IDEA

COMPLAINTS

Dial 'E' for Executive

A PR tactic worth considering: **list the home phone numbers of your company's directors and officers in your catalog.**

That's what Multiplex, a beverage-dispensing equipment maker based in Ballwin, Mo., does. Even with catalogs going out to customers in 75 countries, the $28-million Multiplex lists the numbers of all 16 of its directors in its mailings—along with an invitation to call in case of emergency, if satisfaction can't be had from an area manager.

"The secret," confides chairman and CEO J.W. Kisling, "is we only get a couple of calls a year. But seeing it in writing impresses the hell out of our customers."

90
IDEA

Minimizing Double Trouble

Some customers just seem to attract problems. It's Murphy's Law, says Neil Cannon, CEO of Schmidt-Cannon, a $15-million distributor of promotional items, in City of Industry, Calif. If something goes wrong with their order once, something will go wrong with it twice.

To minimize cases of double errors, Schmidt-Cannon's staff developed a system to **track orders from customers with past problems**. Whenever the company receives a complaint, that customer's next order is placed in a red file to alert the staff to take extra care. When the folder passes through each department, the manager signs off on it personally. If a problem arises, it's the manager who takes responsibility, talking directly with the customer.

In the first three years after the system was put in place, the incidence of repeat complaints dropped noticeably, reports Cannon. At that time, the company was processing about 6,000 orders per month. "We do everything we can to make sure customers are happy," says Cannon. "This way, we can be pretty positive that we've done our job."

91
IDEA

COMPLAINTS

Bigger Bonus for Better Service

How do you get employees to go the extra mile for complaining customers?

One way is to **base a part of their compensation on customer evaluations** of their performance. Renex, a 15-year-old manufacturer of computer peripherals, in Woodbridge, Va., does just that with the employees in its customer-communications center. An administrator contacts customers who have called in with problems and asks them about the performance of the company and its customer-service representatives. The administrator uses the answers to calculate scores for the employees who handled the problem. Scores are averaged quarterly, producing ratings used to determine quarterly bonuses. Bonuses can account for as much as 25% of employees' overall compensation.

The system gives technical support staff the drive to keep doing their best for customers, say company execs. Renex also claims that its typical service rep winds up making about 10% more than the industry average.

COMPLAINTS

The Customer-Complaint Form

Electronic Controls Co. (ECCO), in Boise, Idaho, had a great system for dealing with customer complaints. Customer-service reps, who fielded complaint calls, were authorized to issue credit memos, ship replacement products or parts overnight, or do whatever else was necessary to placate customers. But the process had one drawback: there was no record of the complaints or the reps' responses. "We sensed we were getting the same complaints over and over, but we weren't sure," says ECCO president Ed Zimmer, who was the sales and marketing director at the time.

The solution: ECCO's customer-service team came up with a form to capture the **core data about complaints and the corrective action taken**. A "corrective-action team" then looks at the most common comments and searches out root problems.

By keeping track of each complaint, ECCO has been better able to figure out steps it can take for incremental improvement. For instance, when the company discovered that 33 people complained in one 12-month period about shipments that were either over or under the right quantity, ECCO redesigned its packing slips and added a second check of each box before it gets sealed. Complaints tapered off.

93
IDEA

COMPLAINTS

Standing Out in a Cast of Thousands

Industries like plumbing, heating, and contracting are highly fragmented. They're made up of a lot of small, "son-and-pop" enterprises, all vying for neighborhood business.

How can a company stand out? Larry Harmon of DeMar Plumbing, Heating & Air-conditioning, in Clovis, Calif., says he grew his business from $200,000 in 1985 to $3.2 million in 1993 by solving customers' problems beyond their clogged drains.

That meant first **polling his customers to learn their biggest complaints**. What he heard was that people most hated not knowing when help would arrive and receiving bills that far surpassed job estimates. Harmon set out to solve those problems by introducing guaranteed one-day service and a flat-rate pricing system that covers more than 85% of DeMar's jobs.

He has since added a one-year guarantee on all work and requires that his employees be thoroughly trained in customer satisfaction. DeMar employees also wear uniforms, and the company has a policy of following up service calls with customer surveys.

III

"Managing creative people is an
oxymoron. You don't manage
them at all. Instead you provide
an environment in which they
can be simultaneously
stimulated and protected,
challenged and encouraged,
exposed and private. Day-to-day,
month-to-month 'management'
can be measured in its quality
by its perceived absence."

NICHOLAS NEGROPONTE
professor of media technology,
Massachusetts Institute of Technology
and author of *Being Digital* (Knopf, 1995)

94
IDEA

BENEFITS

Six Weeks with Pay, Period

O ne of a start-up's few luxuries is the freedom employees have to administer the time they take off for sick days, personal days, and vacations. With a small staff, peer pressure alone tends to limit the danger that the freedom will be abused. But what do you do when the company grows? Most companies start policing employees, but when Gary Mokotoff was running a technology company, he created an alternative, which he called flex-leave.

Under the system, employees got six weeks off with pay during the year, which included time for vacation, holidays, family needs, and sickness. **"Every day you didn't come in was counted toward the six weeks**," says Mokotoff. If people used less than the entire six weeks, they got paid for the balance with a bonus.

The policy eliminated abuses of sick time, says Mokotoff, who's now president of the Association of Jewish Genealogical Societies, in Teaneck, N.J. The policy also ended controversy over whether the company should grant vacation time for religious holidays such as Good Friday and Rosh Hashanah.

95

IDEA

Give Benefits to Part-Timers

H oward Schultz, CEO and chairman of Seattle-based Starbucks Coffee, believes his business couldn't achieve profitable growth if it didn't provide competitive employee benefits. In 1990, he began providing all employees, which at the time numbered 1,800, with a benefits package that included stock options, medical and dental insurance, and a free pound of coffee each week. The big surprise was that the program extended to part-time workers, who made up 50% of the company's retail sales force.

Schultz believes such comprehensive benefits coverage is not only feasible but ultimately profitable for growing companies of all sizes. "Including part-timers does increase our insurance fees, but you can't just consider that fact in isolation," says Schultz. **Providing part-timers with insurance has helped bring turnover to below 50%** in an industry where it typically runs more than 100% annually. "Thanks to lower turnover, we've saved more in training costs than we've spent on insurance," notes Schultz, who believes part-timers can become as committed to a company as full-time workers.

In 1992, Starbucks went public. In 1994, it had systemwide sales of $285 million. Part-timers who work more than 20 hours a week still get benefits and stock options.

96
IDEA

BENEFITS

Junk the Company-Car Policy

Buying company cars for sales and service people is a trap, warns Stephen Albano, founder and president of Offtech, a distributor of office equipment, in Wilmington, Mass. "Once you start buying cars, you can't get out of it," he says. His advice: **pay your staff a premium to use their own cars instead**.

Offtech personnel, including 60-plus salespeople and 140 technicians, get paid a flat fee plus 10¢ per mile for on-the-job use of their own cars. Most people, Albano professes, actually prefer to use their own cars rather than drive a model chosen by the company. The system saves the company the cost of having to buy or lease scores of vehicles, not to mention the costs of maintenance and insurance.

The system has also eliminated a potential source of bad morale: the used company car. "How would you feel," asks Albano, "if, on your first day on the job, you got stuck with a 45,000-mile company car that needs new tires and has a rip in the seat?"

97

IDEA

• MANAGING PEOPLE •

Give Out Keys to the Store

One cheap way to bolster your benefits package is to **allow employees to use the company's facility and equipment in off-hours**. Literally giving trusted employees the keys to the store is an old-fashioned gesture of trust that fosters loyalty in these times of diminishing fidelity to workplaces.

At Edson Corp., in New Bedford, Mass., president Will Keene has given seven of the 25 workers keys to the family-owned machine shop, which makes steering systems for yachts. "These people have been with the company at least five years," says Keene. "They aren't out to rip us off." Newer employees get the message that long-term commitment is rewarded.

And the keys are used. Employees can work on their own projects in the shop on weekends, as long as someone else is present in case of injury. The policy means a lot, says Keene, particularly for workers who don't have their own shops.

98
IDEA

BENEFITS

Banking Benefits for Cheap

With a little help from its bank, Eli's Chicago's Finest Cheesecake has been able to **extend its limited benefits resources**.

The $15-million company works with its lender, Columbia National Bank, in Chicago, to offer low-cost banking services for workers in its commercial bakery and restaurant. The bank runs a program called Partnership in Banking, a package of discounted and free services offered through companies to employees. It encourages the use of direct-deposit paycheck services and gives workers free checking accounts, better interest rates on savings accounts, and discounts on loans. The program helps the bank cement relationships with corporate clients. Other banks offer similar programs.

Eli's, though, has taken the program a step further. President Marc Schulman knew that many of the company's employees did without bank accounts, paying exorbitant fees instead for storefront check-cashing services. He asked Columbia to teach his work force how to handle checking accounts, certificates of deposit, and consumer loans. Bank specialists led the classes at no charge.

99
IDEA

BENEFITS

PC's for the Home Front

I f your employees use computers off the job, they'll probably use them better at work. At least that's the thinking at Multiplex, a beverage-dispenser manufacturer, in Ballwin, Mo., which **offers staffers financing on their home computers**, without interest and at substantial savings, to encourage computer literacy.

The deal costs Multiplex little. When the $28-million company buys equipment for its offices, it passes along the bulk discount to employees. They pay 10% down and cover the balance with monthly installments deducted from their paychecks. The only cost to Multiplex is the finance charge on the money it fronts employees for the machines.

Of the company's 65 office workers, more than half have already made purchases. Chairman J.W. Kisling says that he's convinced the program not only improves technical skills inside the company but also boosts employee morale.

1OO IDEA

BENEFITS

Weekend Rewards

I t pays to recharge not just your own batteries, but those of employees as well. At least that's what Joseph and Laurie Cherry have found. Their business, Cherry Tire Service, in Maybrook, N.Y., is a truck-tire road-service company. To show appreciation for the extraordinary efforts their employees give all year long, the Cherrys give an annual, all-expenses-paid **weekend in the Poconos to every long-term employee**. Says Joe Cherry: "When they come back, they are different people."

Everyone who has worked two years or more at Cherry Tire is entitled to take a spouse to Caesars Pocono Resorts, in Lakeville, Pa., where the company provides the couple with a suite for the weekend. Each year an employee returns, the company upgrades the suite—right up to the Champagne Towers with a hot tub shaped like a seven-foot champagne glass. "The upgrading gives everybody something new to look forward to," says Joe Cherry.

The benefit reflects the Cherrys' approach to management. "These guys work very hard at dangerous jobs," says Joe Cherry. "The reason they work hard is that they want a better life. We owe them a salary, just like they owe us the work, but the weekend is different. We're saying, 'This weekend is for you. Take it.' It's worth more psychologically than the money it costs."

101 IDEA

Real-Life Seminars

Looking for a low-cost benefit to offer your employees? Hemmings Motor News, a publisher in Bennington, Vt., holds a series of **on-site seminars for its more than 100 employees** to help them manage their lives better.

A volunteer health team arranges the brown-bag lunchtime talks, drawing ideas from companywide surveys and employees' evaluations of previous seminars. Topics have included low-fat cooking, nutrition for kids, personal investing, weight control, and menopause. Most sessions are free, and for others that require a speaker who charges more than $100, Hemmings charges attendees a small fee. Even then, the cost to the worker is 50% reimbursable under the company's innovative "fitness benefit," which pays for any fitness expense the employee chooses, from joining a health club to buying a bicycle.

Hemmings's philosophy? "The company gains much from energetic, healthy employees," states the company handbook.

102 IDEA

COMMUNICATION

Surveys of Substance

E mployee surveys often carry the risk of becoming excuses for griping instead of tools for change. Getting constructive responses requires careful **design and administration of a questionnaire**—and, of course, good follow-through. Here are some recommendations:

- Ask workers to edit your drafts. To provide honest responses, employees must interpret questions the same way you do. Workers at Just Desserts, a $13-million bakery, in San Francisco, help managers edit out manipulative or leading questions.

- Use descriptive cover letters. Just Desserts introduces surveys with a letter that spells out the survey's purpose. The letter also guarantees that responses will remain confidential. To help ensure privacy, the company hires an outsider to crunch data.

- Do surveys on company time. That's standard for the 800 employees at Wild Oats Market, a 12-store chain, based in Boulder, Colo. "If they do it on their own time, you can get skewed results, what with squeaky wheels and overly cheery new hires," says Wild Oats co-founder Michael Gilliland.

- Leave generous room for suggestions and comments. "The most important changes we made to our profit-sharing plan came out of white space," says Jerry Rackley, product manager at Teubner & Associates, a $4-million software developer, in Stillwater, Okla.

103
IDEA

Solving Interdepartmental Short Circuits

Companies exploding in size should always look for ways to ensure that communication between departments stays open. Work groups tend to become more insular as they grow and to have less interaction with other groups.

When SynOptics Communications, in Santa Clara, Calif., was four years old and had gone from 11 to 425 employees, it faced the communication dilemma. So CEO Andrew Ludwick began holding formal **staff-to-staff lunches**.

Each quarter, the company bought lunch for two of the company's five divisions. People from both groups would sit down at five tables. Each table was given a problem to solve over lunch and present to the rest of the group. "On a superficial level, we were simply solving problems," says Ludwick. "But we also were creating chemistry among all our employees."

Ludwick knows about creating chemistry: in 1994, SynOptics went on to merge with Wellfleet Communications, the top-ranking company on the 1993 *Inc.* 100 list of public companies. The newly formed company, called Buy Networks, is a $1-billion-plus operation—with Ludwick as its CEO.

104
IDEA

Plant an Accountability Tree

As a company grows, it can become tough to keep track of who's responsible for what. "You have people constantly crossing functional lines," says Thomas G. Kamp, whose Premier Computer, formerly of Oklahoma City, grew in four years from 25 people to 260. "It becomes easy for accountability to get lost."

That was hard on management. "I found myself not knowing who was responsible for ensuring proper turnaround time," says Kamp. So he devised a **system for tracking each employee's accountability**. At least once a year, all managers drew up a matrix specifying their responsibilities and those of each of the people under them. The matrix looked like this: Across the top, employees' initials served as column headings. Down the side were different job tasks (such as internal growth planning) and limits of authority (such as being able to approve purchases of up to $500). After all the matrices were complete, they were distributed in loose-leaf binders. "It's a reference tool," says Kamp.

There was another, equally important, payoff from the exercise. "By writing something down, people came to own it," he says.

Cultural Exchanges

A company roster can reflect a wide range of personalities—buttoned-up managers, technology-minded software engineers, flamboyant copywriters. Some managers keep their creative teams all but separate from their business side. Integrated Genetics, however, takes a different course. Living up to its name, the multi-million bioengineering company, in Framingham, Mass., **integrates its business and creative divisions** with regularly scheduled informal talks and seminars.

Every Friday, for instance, one of the scientists gives a presentation to the company at large on subjects ranging from in-house work to new developments in the industry. Once a month an employee from sales, marketing, or administration takes a turn speaking to the scientists on issues like finance and strategic planning. The company also runs a weekly in-house seminar called "Science for Nonscientists," in which scientists explain their work in detail to administrative employees.

"It prevents the scientists from becoming an esoteric group shut off from the company," says a sales and marketing exec. "The formation of corporate cliques, with their own little cultures, is a danger at companies like ours."

106 IDEA

COMMUNICATION

Using Voice Mail All Day Long

Do you **use your company's voice mail for all that it's worth**? You probably don't use it as much as Fred DeLuca, cofounder and president of Subway, the sandwich chain, based in Milford, Conn., that racked up 1994 revenues of $2.7 billion. DeLuca uses Subway's voice-mail system as a tool for constant communication, sending out, he says, an average of four and as many as ten group messages a day to his salespeople.

When, for instance, he hears about something a competitor is doing, he'll pass the information along to everyone, by either summarizing the news he received or forwarding the actual voice message sent to him. "People file it away and maybe don't do anything that minute, but as they learn, they become that much sharper," says DeLuca. "I envision the system as a seminar room."

His typical message, he says, is about one minute long. And he prefers this way of keeping in touch to electronic mail. "A voice conveys emotion," he observes. DeLuca's staff, meanwhile, has learned that if they leave him a message, it's likely to be passed on to their colleagues.

COMMUNICATION

Hone Your Own Handbook

There comes a time in every company's growth when an employee manual becomes essential. "Whether they are explicit or not, companies already have policies in place," says lawyer Robert J. Nobile, a partner at Epstein Becker & Green, in New York City, and author of a guide to handbooks. The act of writing a manual solidifies those policies.

But to get the most out of the process, **the handbook's development should be an inside job**. Kingston Technology, the Fountain Valley, Calif., company that topped the *Inc.* 500 list of fastest-growing private companies in 1992, commissioned a handbook when it reached 75 employees. But, according to marketing director Ron Seide, the hired hand merely took a competitor's handbook, called up the search-and-replace function on the word-processing program, and spat out a revised edition.

Kingston employees hated it. "It contained all this legal butt-covering language, which made it seem as if the company didn't trust us and we didn't trust them," says Carol Ruprecht, who works in international sales. When she told the owners how bad the handbook was, they authorized her to fix it. Ruprecht and her sister, who works in marketing, met with the two founders to get their input and philosophy on issues such as sick leave. The 20-page manual they wrote, all agree, better captures the company's true spirit.

108
IDEA

COMMUNICATION

Putting a Name to a Face

As businesses grow and staffs get bigger, managers know less and less about each employee. What's more, even employees don't know much about one another. One way to attack the problem and celebrate people at the same time is to put together **a company yearbook**.

That's what Copy America (née: Original Copy Centers) did when its staff first reached 110 people working three different shifts. The execution was simple: everybody filled out questionnaires asking about their favorite music, ideal weekend, biggest challenges, and happiest childhood memory. Other fill-in-the-blanks included "What I really like about my job" and "My role at Original." The book devoted a full page, including a photo, to each person.

While the yearbook was for employees, it was also displayed in the lobby of the company's Cleveland headquarters, for customers to browse. And managers used the profiles as background before annual reviews. Cost of production? About $1,600, although most of the work was done in-house.

Handbooks That Won't Haunt You

Just because state courts have been treating policy statements in employee handbooks as binding contracts between companies and employees, you don't need to forgo handbooks altogether. They can be an effective way to communicate values and standards, and **careful drafting will help you avoid most legal problems**. Here are four key do's and don'ts.

- Don't make strong promises. Instead of saying the company "will provide" or "will guarantee" something, say "the company will, whenever practical, provide." Avoid using "guarantee" altogether.

- Don't use phrases like "permanent employee"—they can lead to disputes over terminations.

- At the beginning and end of the handbook, do include a disclaimer to the effect that "this is not a contract. It can be modified at any time."

- Do review the handbook regularly and eliminate outdated rules.

110
IDEA

COMMUNICATION

Cutting Down on 'Us vs. Them'

Even when his company, Oil Changers, was small, Larry Read recognized the danger of dissension in the ranks. That's even more of a danger now that Oil Changers has grown to more than 500 workers, most of whom do automobile lube jobs far removed from front offices.

So from the beginning, Read made it company policy to have blue-collar and white-collar employees mix. Everyone at the company's Pleasanton, Calif., headquarters, including managers, starts by doing lube jobs in the pit. And **everyone in the corporate offices revisits the shop floor one day each month** to greet customers and work on a team, performing non-technical tasks. Read himself works in the field two days a month.

"This is not some fraternal initiation," Read says. The monthly visits make it easier for workers to approach the office with problems. To Read, that alone makes it worth paying someone an executive salary to pop drain plugs for a day. Another benefit is that management can run reality checks on ivory-tower assumptions. While washing windows one day, one cost-conscious executive discovered that the new towels he'd thought would save $20,000 weren't good at absorbing.

111

IDEA

Tell It Like It Was

Lou Bucelli never took his medical-video-production company's growth for granted. Since its bootstrapping days, in 1989, CME Conference Video, in Mount Laurel, N.J., has grown to $9 million in sales, but Bucelli has vivid memories of the lean years, when three people did everything from answering phones to shoveling snow. He wasn't so sure, though, that newer employees understood CME's humble beginnings and the importance of that legacy.

CME now occupies 16,000 square feet and brings in $35,000 a day, but back when the company had 800 square feet, Bucelli was happy to do $300 a day. To get that point across, Bucelli one day gathered the company's 20 employees for a staff meeting in an 800-square-foot roped-off area of the warehouse, and the three **original employees told war stories of the past**. Bucelli also played corporate demo tapes from the company's infancy to show how the focus of CME's work had evolved. The point was to get people's imaginations running.

"If people can look back and say, 'This is how things were at $1 million in sales,' then they can start making a mental vision of how the company will look going forward," Bucelli says.

REAL
WORLD

"Technology doesn't get
enough credit for being the
feminist's friend.
Technology has killed
hierarchy. When you get
into companies that have
E-mail systems, you don't
have to be the loudest
man or the biggest braggart.
It flattens gender
differences."

HARRIET RUBIN
executive editor, Currency/Doubleday,
in New York City

1IDEA**12**

Friday Is E-Mail Update Day

As companies get bigger and more employees go in more directions, it can be difficult to keep a handle on how projects are progressing. One way to stay in touch while trying to flatten the structure of the company is to **ask staff to write short electronic mail updates of their work each week**.

At Indus Group, a management-software company, in San Francisco, all 250 employees input one-page summaries each Friday, outlining what they worked on that week, what their plans are for the coming week, and what impediments they've run into. The packet is posted on the electronic bulletin board for anyone to read.

One person who reads all the summaries is CEO Bob Felton, who also responds to many of them. "It helps short-circuit what happens in hierarchies, where you're not allowed to go and talk to someone," says Felton, who did stints in the navy and as a *Fortune* 500 exec before starting Indus. "And because people have to do it, it's not like they have to take a risk to go around a chain of command. It's what we expect."

113
IDEA

COMPENSATION

Trade Complaints for Challenges

Rick Hartsock remembers when a worker came to him and told him that the pay system at Sandstrom Products, a specialty-coatings manufacturer that Hartsock had just bought, stunk. Hartsock had thought the pay system was pretty good. So he asked the worker, whose problem did he think it should be? The guy was silent. "He said, 'I don't know. I don't know what you're getting at. It's certainly not my problem,'" recalls Hartsock, who asked the employee if anybody else felt the way he did. A lot of people, the worker told him.

Hartsock decided to **let the disgruntled workers come up with a pay plan that would work better** for the $6-million business. He told the worker to get those people together and form a pay-plan committee, and that he would approve any reasonable plan the committee proposed. The ad-hoc group spent seven months developing a new, customized pay-for-knowledge system, which the company promptly implemented. Now the 36 employeees of the Port Byron, Ill., company work up from $10 to $15 an hour by learning new skills.

Let Employees Set Pay Rates

With 100 employees, Com-Corp Industries, a metal-stamping shop, in Cleveland, is an open-book company where employees earn not only above-market wages but a share of the profits. Turnover is less than 5% annually, and the company has earned better-than-industry-average profits most years. One key to Com-Corp's success: **putting major compensation decisions into the hands of employees**.

Ten to 15 employees volunteer to serve on the company's Wage and Salary Committee for two-year stints. The committee surveys and collects job-skills data and wage information from comparable companies in the region. That information determines the pay scales. Then managers review employee performance, based on measurable criteria such as parts produced per hour and safety compliance as well as soft criteria such as how well a worker gets along with others. If an employee scores 80%, his or her pay will be 80% of the highest rate of pay for that particular job.

There are checks and balances, too. Peers report on how their colleagues are doing, and the human-resources director can step in to reevaluate an appraisal. Workers are also free to conduct their own compensation-rate surveys and bring their findings and requests to an employee-run Human Resources Assistance Committee.

115
IDEA

COMPENSATION

Spell Out the Whole Story

Small, growing companies usually can't pay their people as much as larger outfits down the street. But your company will look better if you **let employees know exactly how much their full package is worth**—not just salary, but health insurance, workers' comp, 401(k) contributions, parking, and so on.

For instance, while employers know that insurance and other benefit costs are exploding, employees often don't understand just how high the true cost of keeping them on the payroll is. American Teleconferencing Services, in Overland Park, Kans., is one of many companies that send out a one-page accounting, along with its W-2 forms, that details what the company spent on the employee in addition to wages or salary, including the cost of company parties and outings, training, and other perks.

Doug Greene, founding CEO of New Hope Communications, a Boulder, Colo., publisher, says he's convinced his disclosure makes it easier to control costs. In giving raises, for instance, he can tell an employee that he or she is getting a 4% raise in pay and a 7% increase in benefits, which helps emphasize the constraints the business is operating under.

FIRING

Staying Out of Court

Employment litigation has exploded. Discrimination lawsuits, which have risen by more than 2,200% over the past two decades, now account for an estimated one-fifth of all civil suits filed in U.S. courts. In large part, the suits have come since 1989, when courts in 45 states accepted several theories that eroded the "at will" principle, which allowed employers to fire someone for any reason, as long as it wasn't discriminatory or in violation of a collective-bargaining agreement. Now, employers have become subject to so-called implied contracts, under which job rights may be inferred when no explicit contract exists.

The best protection against lawsuits is to **institute a clear and diligent system of evaluating, documenting, and taking action** with employees. For example, at Community Bank of Homestead, in greater Miami, "if an employee does something significant enough that it could result in termination, the manager documents it and sits down with the individual," says Marlene Porter, human-resources director. The process "sets a time limit—usually 30 to 90 days—for shortcomings to be corrected. If the situation is no better after that, you sit down with the employee again, and you warn the person that there will not be a third counseling session." The key is documentation. "I did have to terminate someone," says bank credit manager Roberta Greaves, "and there was talk of legal action. But because we had full documentation, nothing came of it."

117
IDEA

FIRING

What Lawyers Love to Find

Firing an employee is never fun, but being sued in the aftermath makes it worse. According to Lonny H. Dolin of Dolin & Modica, in Rochester, N.Y., you'll look bad in court if an employee can show:

- A personnel file that, after the fact of termination, is "papered" with memos written from memory.
- Training for new or younger workers but not for older employees—like giving some people time off to attend seminars but not others.
- Different working terms and conditions among employees with comparable skills.
- Conflicting records performance. An example: a subordinate is told his project isn't good and ultimately is terminated, but the performance review for the superior lauds the same project.

IDEA

Tape Your Interviews

Concerned about your interviewing techniques? One piece of advice from personnel consultant Ed Ryan, of MPR, in Chicago, is to **audiotape job interviews**.

Ryan says candidates answer more thoughtfully and honestly when they know you're recording every word (you must, by law, ask interviewees' permission before you start taping). What's more, says Drew Conway, CEO of the Registry, a provider of computer-literate workers, in Newton, Mass., taping has improved his own interviewing techniques. He began to notice how much talking instead of listening *he* did, and he learned to ask more open-ended questions, which elicit more than yes or no responses. He also trained himself to ask for examples.

It's imperative that you treat all applicants the same. If you tape one interview, you must tape them all, or else you could be accused of discrimination. Indeed, the tapes may protect you from unfounded claims of discrimination by providing proof of equal treatment in hiring.

119
IDEA

<u>HIRING</u>

Reach the Pros with House Calls

You'll always do better looking for new hires if you focus your search. Accu Bite Dental Supply, a 29-employee dental-products distributor, in Williamston, Mich., gave up on using classified ads and recruitment agencies to find employees because they were too scattershot. Instead, the company rents mailing lists from local dental-profession organizations and **sends job notices to prospective employees' homes**. For each opening, Accu Bite sends about 500 letters. It receives a 5% to 6% response.

120
IDEA

Hardball Interviewing

Most CEOs aren't as hardcore about hiring as Richard Rose of Dataflex, but then most CEOs can't boast a sales force that routinely outsells its industry average by a factor of 10.

To join the sales staff at Dataflex, a $275-million public company that sells computer equipment and services and regularly appears on best-managed-company lists, candidates go through grueling in-your-face interviews with Rose. His goal is to find people with confidence in their abilities, a willingness to take calculated risks, a great sense of humor, and nimble thinking.

Rose's assistant is instructed to give the brush-off to people who call the company's Edison, N.J., headquarters answering a Dataflex ad. Only those who are persistent and insist that they're worth Rose's time clear the first hurdle. Then, says Rose, "**I am deliberately adversarial in the first interview.**" He puts candidates on the spot, tests their convictions, and tries to see how honest they are about things like being motivated by money. He looks for honesty, tenacity, and thickness of skin. "If they're too sensitive, they aren't going to do well around here." Rose, who cowrote a book about his tactics (*How to Make a Buck and Still Be a Decent Human Being*, HarperBusiness, 1992), concludes interviews by telling candidates to call him after they've thought the job over. "About half never work up the nerve," he reports.

121
IDEA

HIRING

Man on the Street

When you need entry-level employees, one way to find them is embarrassingly simple: **consider everyone you meet in passing a potential staff member**. One company that used this guerrilla strategy found and hired eight people, who worked out for the business. In one case, when the CEO's car broke down during a late-night snowstorm, a sympathetic off-duty taxi driver interrupted his coffee break to take him home. The CEO responded by offering him a job as a driver for the company, which the cabbie ended up taking.

Another way to meet potential employees is to forgo the self-serve pump at gas stations. Unpinched pennies at the pump rewarded the same CEO with an especially courteous attendant who was ready to switch jobs.

Finding Their Own Replacements

Having employees hire the people they'll be working with can be the best way to ensure that teams function well together. At Johnsonville Foods, a manufacturer in Sheboygan, Wis., **employees who are promoted from merchandisers to salespeople hire their replacements**. Merchandisers and salespeople work closely together, with merchandisers backing up the sales force. Because so much of salespeople's compensation comes from performance bonuses, their hiring decisions affect dramatically how much money they end up making.

"I want people to learn how to get good people, how to coach them, and what it takes to get good performance," says CEO Ralph Stayer. "They'll also learn lessons in bad hiring early on at a level where mistakes are chicken feed to the company."

123
IDEA

HIRING

Home Away from Home

I f you're having trouble finding good people because of a tight local labor market, you may have to start recruiting farther afield. But how far? And where?

Bread Loaf Construction, in Middlebury, Vt., had good luck by **targeting its search for employees** to geographic areas with not only a depressed market but also a similar climate. At the 100-employee business, in the heart of New England's ski region, managers considered both Denver and Houston as possible recruitment sites when the construction market was flat in both cities. They chose Denver, however, in hopes of appealing to already ski-happy people who might be eager to relocate.

It worked. A newspaper advertisement garnered a flood of resumés, and during a two-day visit to Denver, then-vice-president John Leehman interviewed more than two dozen people. Ultimately, the company hired four. Two years later, two of them were still with the company; "for the cost of a hotel room, a plane ticket, and 30% of their relocation costs, it was worth it," says Leehman.

IDEA 124

Getting to the Truth

The litigation explosion has made it harder to get **candid references for job applicants**, as former employers grow nervous about possible lawsuits from their ex-employees. But there are things you can do to improve your chances of getting accurate information, reports Peter LeVine, of Framingham, Mass., who has built a business as a professional reference checker:

- Keep your questions neutral, so you don't offend anyone or lead the reference. Don't ask, "Does she buckle under pressure?" but rather, "How does she handle pressure?"
- Avoid mentioning the job until you've discussed the applicant. Otherwise, the reference may focus on the position, not the person.
- Don't just talk to the applicant's previous boss. Often the best information comes from peers and outsiders, such as suppliers, customers, or auditors.
- Check academic and previous job credentials. "If the candidate has lied about that," says LeVine, "I'll guarantee he or she has lied about things you can't verify."

125 IDEA

HIRING

Postinterview Interviews

When you're hoping to make a hire, you need as much information as you can get. One way to add another piece to a profile is to **have applicants write up "minutes" after a job interview**. Victoria B. Buyniski, founder, CEO, and president of $11-million United Medical Resources, in Cincinnati, has used the approach to hire 75% of the 189 associates who staff her managed-care business.

Candidates who don't come off well in a face-to-face interview get a second chance to show off their attributes in their writing, says Buyniski. On the other hand, others describe a job markedly different from what the company has to offer, indicating potential communication problems. Candidates can use computers to write up the minutes, which shows what kind of word-processing programs they are familiar with.

"Three pages dashed off in 15 minutes tells me they are producers," says Buyniski.

126
IDEA

When Employees Want to Leave

It's frustrating when you make a good hire, train a talented person, and then find out he or she is leaving. Sometimes a manager's first reaction when an employee gives notice is anger. But that's the wrong attitude, says Jeffrey Mount, president of Wright's Gourmet House, a $2-million restaurant and catering company, in Tampa. He says the question's not *if* they're leaving, but *when*.

"People burn out and move on," says Mount, who has 36 employees. "Hard as it is, when staff members give notice, I don't try to stop them. I thank them for their contributions and wish them well." If it's a person he really values, he leaves the door open for them to return. Often they do.

The key thing is to **recognize that people will leave and to plan for it**, anticipate it, suffer it, and live with it. "After years of whining about people's leaving, I've come to believe that a resignation letter is good news for everyone involved," says Mount, because unless some staff members are in transition, neither the organization nor its people are growing.

127
IDEA

Beware of Hiring Questions

Suppose you're a retailer and you need to hire a salesperson who speaks Spanish fluently. In the course of interviewing a candidate, you ask, "So, where did you learn to speak Spanish?" Watch out. According to the Equal Employment Opportunity Commission, you may have just committed an act of discrimination.

Most job seekers won't haul you to court over such an inquiry, but **it pays to stay informed**. One source: *Essential Facts: Employment,* published by Warren, Gorham & Lamont (800-950-1205, $95 plus shipping and tax). This book covers issues including the Americans with Disabilities Act, pre-employment testing, workplace violence, and employee privacy.

HIRING

Tapping the Big Boys

When you're looking for top employees, try checking in with the human-resources departments of larger corporations in your area that may have had recent layoffs. Some send out **free books filled with ex-employees' resumés**, from hard-to-find experienced factory-floor workers to research-and-development engineers.

When Eric Giler, president of Brooktrout Technology, a maker of electronic-messaging systems, in Needham, Mass., was first growing the now-public company, that's how he found employees. Brooktrout went from 20 to 40 people in six months, and five engineers came in via recommendations from local corporations. "It's tough to get hired by those companies," says Giler. "They've done a first cut for us." Giler also estimates that by not using a corporate headhunter, the company saved $30,000.

129 IDEA

HIRING

Get Applicants to Check Up on You

David Blumenthal puts his own spin on reference checking: **he insists that serious job candidates call the *company's* own references** to get a true picture of Flash Creative Management, his information-technology company, in River Edge, N.J. "Call these people, and they'll tell you the type of company you're getting involved with," he instructs them. "No holds barred on questions."

References usually are Flash's customers, who often end up providing a second set of interviews for Blumenthal. He'll check if the candidate asked intelligent questions and if the customer would feel comfortable working with that person. The process also reveals prospective employees' willingness to take direction as well as the strength of their interest in Flash, a $2-million business.

"It's the first manifestation of their relationship with the company," says Blumenthal. "If I ask them to call references and they don't, I get a different message."

REAL WORLD

"The secret of business, especially these days, is to focus relentlessly on your unfair advantage—the thing you do that others don't. Mindful of that focus, you decide on specific objectives and on the division of labor needed to achieve them. Plenty of debate may precede the setting of those goals, but in the end everyone signs on. Which makes business an essentially exclusionary enterprise, not an inclusionary one. Anybody is welcome to join as long as he or she agrees with exactly what we're for. If you don't agree, please don't come: go do something else."

JOHN ROLLWAGEN
former CEO of Cray Research,
in Eagan, Minn

130
IDEA

Tap Youthful Enthusiasm

If you're not using student interns, you're missing a huge opportunity, says Patrick Daw, president of $1.4-million Triad LLC, in Glastonbury, Conn. Because they regard the sponsoring company as a potential employer, interns "want to take the job a step farther," observes Daw, who finds them "dedicated, solid, and dependable."

Internships also help promising students develop specific skills before they start asking to join the staff permanently. Walter Joseph Communications, a Chicago video-production company, has hired about a third of the 35 to 40 interns who have logged time there.

And there's an ego boost for regular staffers that comes from teaching others their skills. "You get used to what you're doing, and then there's a new, lively person who's in total awe of everything you say and do," says Walter Joseph's Dale Vermillion, vice-president of operations. "They rejuvenate the staff."

131
IDEA

INCENTIVES

Target Incentives by Function

Whatever combination of straight salaries, commissions, and goal-based bonus incentives you use to motivate your staff, it's crucial to make sure you're not inadvertently sending mixed signals about what is and isn't important for your business. Incentives to focus on one thing may unintentionally cause people to ignore other important goals.

When G.O.D. (Guaranteed Overnight Delivery), an express freight service, in Kearney, N.J., first took its dock loaders off hourly wages and paid them for each shipment handled, freight loss and breakage became epidemic. "The system just sped people up," says CEO Walter Riley. "The dock loaders thought, 'If there are mistakes, there are mistakes.'"

The incentive system had to change to **reward specific areas**. Under a new system, loaders still get piecework pay but they are also awarded a weekly bonus of 25% of their week's earnings if all shipments get through with no breakage, misloading, or short cartons.

When the new system was introduced, not only did 85% of workers begin to meet the bonus requirements, but they ended up acting as quality checks for the whole freight-hauling operation as well. Result: companywide productivity improved.

132
IDEA

INCENTIVES

Cash and Kudos in Advance

During busy times, it's great to be able to count on employees giving 100%. One way to create an atmosphere where people really care is to **give out bonuses before the hectic times hit**.

At Winter Gardens Salad, in New Oxford, Pa., peak demand comes right before Memorial Day, when the $60-million food-service firm gets a run on its coleslaw and potato salad. And that's when CEO Harry Seifert hands out $50 to each of the company's 200 employees. "When I give them the money, I tell them we are going for a record to give them something to shoot for," says Seifert. Usually, production for that week is 50% greater than for other weeks. "Because they're trying to achieve a goal, they don't feel as if they are being taken advantage of during the intense week."

Seifert says he purposely reserves the bonus for special occasions. "It's like the 100-yard dash," he says. "You can't expect employees to sprint year-round."

133
IDEA

INCENTIVES

Non-Sales Sales Commissions

t's a common dilemma for a company: salespeople focus on getting as many sales as possible, no matter what kinds of pressure last-minute business puts on the people who have to fulfill the orders. The employees who have to accommodate those sales often have to reprioritize their work and put in overtime. The problem: only the first set of employees gets commissions. The result: resentment The solution? Commissions for all.

That's what Bill Byrne figured out at the regional farming magazine he founded, *Tri-State Neighbor* (his publishing business, Byrne Companies, is based in Sioux Falls, S.D.) Without taking incentives away from his advertising reps, Byrne added incentives for other staffers. For every ad page sold above a base level, the magazine's five production and administrative employees split $20. As the number of ads increases, the monthly shares grow to about $200 a person.

It wasn't free, but **the commission-for-all program helped cut down friction**. Before, says Byrne, production people groaned when ads came in late. With the program, they started pushing salespeople to get out and sell more. And because they wanted their shares to grow, they became less interested in adding new staff.

134
IDEA

INCENTIVES

Bonuses à la Carte

Do you think you know what incentive will motivate your staff? Think again. The prizes that turn on one person may bore another. It doesn't take much time or trouble to ask people what they want to work toward and then **custom design an incentive program for each**.

That's what Kirk Malicki did when he was running Pegasus Personal Fitness. New physical-fitness trainers were asked to make a list of rewards, ranging in value from $25 to $200, that they'd like to receive for reaching weekly and monthly goals. Instead of commonplace prizes, employees opted for rock-concert tickets, limousine rentals, and half-days off.

"They know what motivates them better than I do, so I just ask," says Malicki, who grew Pegasus to six locations in Phoenix and Dallas before selling it.

INCENTIVES

Bonuses for One and All

I t may be heretical, but Dave Jones decided not to pay bonuses to sales-people for bringing in new accounts. His problem was that the system benefited only a handful of people. In 1993, he canned the old bonus system and instituted **a profit-sharing plan that includes everyone**. As CEO of HRStrategies, a $17-million human-resources consulting firm, in Grosse Pointe, Mich., Jones felt that even though not everyone's job directly affects company profits, everyone in a small office has an impact. Each of the company's eight offices is a profit center, rewarded on its own income statement.

To compensate for the fact that some team members work harder than others, each office director can use up to 30% of the profit pot to reward "special players." Otherwise, each individual's bonus is a percentage of salary. And while some salespeople favored the old volume-based sales bonuses and eventually left, most, maintains Jones, were relieved to share responsibility for sales.

136
IDEA

INCENTIVES

Play the Great Game of Business

Over the past decade, a growing number of companies have embraced **the concept of "The Great Game of Business"**—where business is thought of as a game, with every employee a player, and all players are given a stake in winning (and all players are at risk, too). A company sets tangible goals—as basic as recording a profit at the end of the month—and everybody is taught how to track the numbers. The numbers go up on scoreboards, and bonuses are passed out if the targets are hit. The effect of such measures can be electric.

The granddaddy of the idea is Springfield Remanufacturing Corp. (SRC), a midsize engine remanufacturer, in Springfield, Mo. In 1983, SRC, a struggling division of International Harvester (now Navistar), was bought by 13 managers, led by Jack Stack, who soon realized they owned a factory with a doubtful future and a mountain of debt. "What else could we do?" Stack asks rhetorically. "We had to teach people how to make money."

Today, SRC teaches its processes to outsiders through on-site seminars and internally produced books (for more information, call 800-FUN2PLAY). Stack also wrote a book, *The Great Game of Business* (Currency/Doubleday, 1992), which outlines the challenges and payoffs in detail.

137 IDEA

Business as a Horse Race

Turning a company into a "Great Game of Business"—where the company's operations are run like a game, with players, rules, winners, and rewards—isn't easy. But there are simple ways a company can begin. The key is being prepared to reveal the numbers that make games into something more than trivial exercises in employee manipulation.

For instance, Heatway, an $8-million floor-heating-system manufacturer, in Springfield, Mo., sponsors **"Guess-the-Gross" contests**. "We circulate a form like a racing form at the start of every month," explains vice-president Dan Chiles, one of two brothers who run the company, which has 48 employees. "At the bottom is a tip sheet—last month's gross, this month's gross last year, our forecasts, what's on the projections we give the bank." The winner gets $25. But the real purpose, says president and co-owner Mike Chiles, is "focusing people's attention on the bottom line."

138
IDEA

MOTIVATION

No More Workers Anonymous

No one likes to feel like a nameless cog in a company, and that's especially the case with production workers, who often feel anonymous and underappreciated. "It's crucial to break that barrier," says Chet Giermak, CEO and president of Eriez Magnetics, a $50-million manufacturer of magnetic laboratory equipment and metal-detection equipment, in Erie, Pa.

One small step Eriez has taken is to put **nameplates in the factory's work areas**, with each employee's name engraved on a 4-by-30-inch slat. The person's job description is preceded by the word "sales"—as in sales/welding or sales/machine shop—to reinforce the message that they play a role in the company's growth.

"I have a nameplate on my desk," says Giermak, "and these people are every bit as important to the company as I am." People like to see their names up there, he adds. "Everybody wants to feel needed and useful."

MOTIVATION

Celebrate Safe Days

Shop-floor accidents are costly in so many ways—injured employees, lost work time, blips in productivity, increases in workers' compensation insurance—that **when a day goes by without an accident, it's worth celebrating**. Peavey Electronics, in Meridian, Miss., has a novel way of applauding safety track records: it runs an ongoing game of bingo.

The company issues bingo cards to employees. At the end of any day in which there has been no lost time due to accidents, a number is called over the public address system. Making bingo is worth a $100 U.S. savings bond.

Announcing a shift free of accidents emphasizes the importance of safety. And bringing people closer to winning the $100 bond "makes a nice close to the day," reports Melia Peavey, the company's president.

140 IDEA

MOTIVATION

Workplace Basics to Go

How do you engage workers in entry-level jobs? There's no magic answer. Ari Weinzweig, of Zingerman's Delicatessen, in Ann Arbor, Mich., thinks it takes a combination of providing lots of information, listening to ideas and suggestions, and giving staffers a financial stake in the company.

Weinzweig, co-owner of the restaurant and food store, says his primary job is **selling the company's principles to the staff** of 140 people. Week after week, the company reiterates how important those jobs are. Employees receive a hefty monthly newsletter detailing new products, departmental news, and the company's direction. The newsletter also reviews business books. Zingerman's posts weekly sales and labor costs, while at open monthly meetings, management reviews profit-and-loss statements. All employees are eligible for profit sharing after one year.

Zingerman's works to provide opportunities for advancement. Of the 52 senior employees, 44 came from within the ranks. That practice requires more training, but the payoff is worth it, Weinzweig says. The employees already understand the company and its customers, which is the most difficult thing to teach new hires.

REAL
WORLD

"You cannot make business
decisions about competing in
today's world without considering
the people who have to 'buy'
the change and deliver results.
Companies that are reengineering
and then realize they're having
a motivation problem are
only halfway there."

FRAN SUSSNER RODGERS
CEO of Work/Family Directions, in Boston.
Rodgers was *Inc.*'s 1994
Socially Responsible Entrepreneur of the Year

141
IDEA

MOTIVATION

The Montessori Manager

Jim Rosen doesn't mean to be patronizing when he says that the same **techniques he used as a Montessori teacher** 20 years ago have turned out to be effective with the 90 employees of his Petaluma, Calif., dry-soup-mix manufacturing company. It's just that the axioms that worked in the classroom also work in his $28-million company, Fantastic Foods.

"You want people to stretch, but you need to make sure they have the ability and the tools to achieve their goals," says Rosen. Montessori teaches that you never do for children what they can do for themselves. Similarly, Rosen thinks that "if you're a good manager, once your people are up to speed, you never do their jobs for them."

Whenever possible, Rosen also tries to let employees "run with their ideas, even if I think they should go in a different direction. They'll learn something on their own, and that's more powerful than if it comes from me." On the production floor, benchmarks, such as daily production goals, are posted. "It's automatic feedback, and it's impersonal," he says.

"Each person evaluates himself or herself," Rosen emphasizes. "The clarity takes away stress, and we want to get rid of all the stress we can."

Supporting Employees' Outside Lives

The waiters at Philadelphia's White Dog Cafe will never care about their jobs as much as owner Judy Wicks does—White Dog is her life. For many of the waiters, their lives are their art—painting, writing, playing music. Others have families that come first. But instead of ignoring those outside interests, Wicks celebrates them. The cafe holds **an annual "Anniversary Howl,"** at which employees exhibit their art, read their poetry, show their films, explain their volunteer week, and introduce their new babies.

Says Deb Sloane, who has worked at White Dog for five years, "There's no way I could have a straight job and do my painting. At most places, the company comes first. Here, there's a balance."

White Dog employees also participate in a company-run mentoring program for inner-city children and volunteer to help feed homeless people and cook at benefit dinners for community-service agencies. Others have traveled, with the cafe's financial assistance, to sister restaurants in Cuba, Nicaragua, and Romania on cultural exchanges.

White Dog designed its programs for the free spirits that restaurant work attracts. The programs help Wicks fight the turnover endemic to the restaurant industry: more than 25 of 100 employees have been with the company for more than three years, at least 10 have been there for four years, and another handful for more than five years.

143
IDEA

PROFIT SHARING

Partners in Profit

Those who don't own a piece of the company tend to lose little sleep over runaway costs—which is a problem for those who *do* own the company. The best way to get people to care, short of sharing ownership, is to share profits. And some companies find that the benefits of profit sharing are enhanced if it's done monthly.

When Philip Edelstein was running Danbury Plumbing Supply, in Danbury, Conn., he began the habit of posting a chart of the company's gross sales and expenses each month. He also **put 15% of profits into a "mini-bonus" pool**. The bonuses were distributed each month to all 20 employees, using a formula that weighed salary level and seniority. Edelstein says that "about five minutes after I started it," employees began turning out lights and closing doors. Instead of using seven heaters to warm the company's warehouse, staffers used just two. "They knew it would come back to them," says Edelstein.

And it did. One year, the business handed out about $100,000 in mini-bonuses. Meanwhile, employee productivity soared: Danbury's sales per employee were about $400,000, twice the industry average. Edelstein's current business, Creative Bath, also in Danbury, has a similar profit-sharing plan in place.

Passbooks to Profit Sharing

Companies that are generous enough to have a profit-sharing plan ought to be savvy enough to make sure employees understand how much the plan means for them. But a lot of businesses make only one perfunctory profit-sharing announcement annually and don't highlight the returns for each person. "Most companies hand out certificates at the end of the year telling employees how much they've socked away, and it gets stuffed in a drawer and forgotten," says Roy G. Gignac, CEO and president of Engineering Design & Sales (EDS), in Danville, Va.

Instead, his electronic design and manufacturing company issues each eligible employee an **ersatz savings passbook for recording profit-sharing vitals** of company contributions and interest earned. "I wanted my profit sharing to have a more immediate effect on my employees—to be a reason to stay with my company," says Gignac. "And I wanted to make it easy for them to understand how much we're doing for them."

Moreover, EDS gives out profit sharing not once a year, but once a month. The company's accounting department calculates the shares based on the previous month's profits. "Employees can see their hard work pay off on a monthly basis," says Gignac, "which is much more rewarding. And they take a more active interest in the plan."

145
IDEA

PROFIT SHARING

Doling Out Nonequity Ownership

The founders of Outback Steakhouse faced two big challenges when they started the company in 1987: they needed start-up cash, and they wanted to create equity opportunities for the restaurant chain's general managers. They nailed both with one solution: they **asked key employees to invest in the company** in return for a share of the profits they generate.

For signing a five-year contract and investing $25,000, a general manager purchases 10% of the cash flow of his or her restaurant (that's earnings before taxes, interest, depreciation, and amortization). Managers earn a base salary of $45,000, and the formula originally was expected to yield above-average incomes of $60,000 to $80,000 a year. But in the late 1980s, the average Outback restaurant actually made $3.2 million at a 23% margin—which worked out to an extra $73,600 a year per manager. In addition, each general manager receives about 4,000 shares of stock options that vest over a five-year period.

Management turnover industrywide typically runs 30% to 40% a year, but with Outback's five-year contract, its turnover was only 5.4% in 1993. The ownership package has attracted veteran managers. And the Tampa-based company has blossomed: 1993 revenues topped $271 million, and the company's founders were named *Inc.*'s 1994 Entrepreneurs of the Year.

146
IDEA

The Buddy System

High school and college students can be good employees, but their schedules tend to get complicated by schoolwork, athletic events, and new love interests. One way to ensure that their shifts will be covered is to set up a formal buddy system. That's how Lisa C. Renshaw manages her 54 parking lots in Maryland, Virginia, and Washington, D.C.

"For every shift, I **assign two people for each job**," says Renshaw, president of 140-employee Penn Parking, in Linthicum, Md. "You'll have the 2:30 p.m. to 10:30 p.m. shift Monday through Wednesday, and I'll have it Thursday through Sunday, and you and I will be buddies. If I can't cover my shift, I can call you up and switch. And you can do the same for me."

Rarely can both people not make it, says Renshaw. "People are more than willing to cover for their buddies," she says, "because they know that someday they'll want them to return the favor."

147
IDEA

SCHEDULING

Employee Exchange Nixes Layoffs

Faced with more employees than work and the possibility of having to institute layoffs, Ted Castle, president of Rhino Foods, a $5-million specialty dessert maker, in Burlington, Vt., turned to the staff to help think of alternatives. One suggestion: **contract out idle workers to other local businesses**.

Rhino's human-resources director, Marlene Dailey, contacted companies interested in hiring temporary workers. Ice cream manufacturer Ben & Jerry's Homemade, the company's biggest customer, ended up taking on Rhino workers in its production department. Gardener's Supply, a catalog company, used exchange employees to fulfill orders.

Workers received the salaries the other company normally paid for those jobs, unless they were lower than what the worker made at Rhino; in that case, Rhino made up the difference. Paychecks continued to be cut by Rhino, and the company continued paying health and dental benefits as well as workers' comp.

The program had its costs: the money to cover the salary differentials and benefits, plus Dailey and Castle's time over the four weeks it took to set up the trade. But it was less costly, Rhino management believes, than the alternatives of layoffs or trying to come up with make-work.

Home Movies

Contrary to popular opinion, training videos don't have to be expensive to produce or a drag to watch. In fact, sometimes the lower tech the better—especially if the videos are produced by the people who will be watching them.

At Motor Cargo, in North Salt Lake City, a team of eight truckers and a dispatcher produced **an entertaining, informative video for their co-workers** on the less-than-scintillating topic of how to catch billing errors caused by inaccurate shipment descriptions.

Producing the video was a welcome break from routine at the then-$45-million freight company. The team of truckers donated 400 work hours to produce, direct, and act out scenes of billing mistakes, and Motor Cargo paid $1,500 to have the footage edited. The payoff: in a test study, the company saved $16.48 per bill because of more accurate descriptions, and the video soon paid for itself. And because the video was like a home movie, it was the first training video that the staff seemed really excited to watch.

149 IDEA

TRAINING

The IBM Way

Where do entreprenuers come from these days? As often as not, they're trying new careers after stints at corporations that have trimmed back their workforces. Ex-IBM employees, for instance, are starting companies in droves; roughly 15% to 18% of former IBM employees have become entrepreneurs, which is about twice the percentage of all corporate refugees starting businesses.

Having been trained at the biggest of big businesses has prepared these new company founders in surprising ways. For instance, at Timecorp Systems, a software company, in Atlanta, salespeople are taught according to Big Blue code. Rather than hiring one employee at a time, CEO Mike Coles **signs on at least three or four sales staffers at once, so he can train them together** at Timecorp University's four-week symposium. At that intense indoctrination, Timecorp veterans teach newcomers about the company's products and how to sell them. After that, the rookies do an obligatory apprenticeship with the pros. Once they complete training and become salespeople, they fight for corporate prizes; the company cloned IBM's practice of giving trips and recognition to top performers, last year sending 16 of the company's 45 employees on a cruise to the French West Indies.

Coles also writes annual "quota letters" to his salespeople, detailing such goals as how much business he expects them to do in the coming year. He took that tradition directly—and unconsciously—from IBM. "I do that without even thinking about it," he says.

REAL
WORLD

"Managing talented,
creative people
is like herding cats
down the beach."

RICHARD MILLER
former vice-president
at General Magic,
in Sunnyvale, Calif.

150
IDEA

Sponsoring New Hires

First impressions last, which is why it pays to think about how new employees are introduced to your company. The way new hires are handled during their first few weeks on the job goes far toward determining whether they'll become enthusiastic contributors. With that in mind, Sequent Computer Systems decided not to leave anything to chance.

The Beaverton, Ore., company **assigns every new hire a sponsor** before his or her first day of work. The sponsor is charged with introducing the new recruit to others, rounding up office supplies, giving instruction on using the electronic mail system, and generally imparting company culture.

Sponsors volunteer for the assignments and commit about 30 minutes a day to their adoptees over the first couple of weeks. Sequent is convinced that the cost of losing the daily half-hour of labor is far exceeded by the program's benefits. "One of the main values of this company is teamwork," says Barbara Gaffney, vice-president for quality. "New employees work better if they know the other players, and a sponsor is one way they get to know people faster."

151
IDEA

TRAINING

Teach by Example

One of the best ways to make job training bearable is to make it fun. What's more, **a training period that's enjoyable fosters a camaraderie** among newcomers and acclimates them to corporate culture. Joe Crugnale, founder and CEO of Bertucci's, a $103-million chain of 67 pizzerias, says he accomplishes all those things every time he opens a new restaurant.

For the first two weeks of every launch, Crugnale and as many as a dozen managers from the company's Wakefield, Mass., corporate office work side by side with the waiters, bartenders, and dishwashers. Crugnale says that he looks forward to the manual labor after the weeks of tedious paperwork and negotiations before an opening. "We kid around a lot with the new hires, and it breaks up the monotony of the legal stuff for the managers. It's the fun part of opening a restaurant."

Managers of the new restaurants like the arrangement, too. "We know they need help, so we just fill in wherever we can," says Crugnale. As for the message his work sends to employees: "The new hires see us go, go, go, and they work a little harder."

152 IDEA

TRAINING

Portable Consultants

In-house training programs are gradually becoming standard for innovative, growing companies. The programs, though, need not be conventional or expensive. **One efficient way to convey information: books**.

At Pro Fasteners, a hardware distributor, in San Jose, Calif., founder Steve Braccini launched a quality program by giving a paperback copy of Philip Crosby's *Quality Without Tears* (McGraw-Hill, 1984) to everyone, which at the time was about 30 people. The book's simplicity was its virtue. "Everybody could understand it," Braccini says. The company then followed up with two months of weekly discussion groups. Braccini guesses that as many as a quarter of the employees hadn't read the book, but through the discussions, everyone became familiar with the basic concepts of quality.

153
IDEA

Borrow from the Big Guys

Need materials to use for in-house training? Before you try to reinvent the wheel, **ask the big companies you work with if you can borrow their curricula.**

Large companies can be an excellent source of training materials, and it's often in their interest to lend them to you. Unitech Composites, a Hayden Lake, Idaho, manufacturer of composite parts for the aircraft industry, was able to borrow an old blueprint-reading curriculum from Boeing, a customer. It also found that manufacturers like DuPont, which makes one of the materials Unitech uses extensively, are happy to send in technical staff to teach the relevant sections of their training programs.

And when you can't borrow, you at least can share. When Unitech was interested in a management-training course for its managers and supervisors, the price seemed prohibitive. So it joined with three other organizations to split four ways the cost of purchasing the training program.

154
IDEA

TRAINING

Speaking about Education

In cities from Los Angeles to Miami to New York, companies are dealing with employees new to this country, for whom English is not a first language. Some companies take the initiative and set up language classes in-house, but they don't have to do it on their own. **Government programs can help offset the costs of teaching employees English.**

When Tabra, a $4-million jewelry maker, in Novato, Calif., wanted to teach its production employees English as a Second Language (ESL), it got two grants from the state of California to cover the cost of paying an outside instructor. Human-resources manager Joyce Shearer, who found out about the state program through a local literacy council, says that obtaining funding was not complicated. The American Society for Training and Development, in Alexandria, Va., says that all 50 states offer training or tax credits.

The programs pay off. With ESL instruction, Keomany Douangprachant, originally from Laos and an eight-year veteran of Tabra, advanced from her job as an assembler to become a production supervisor. And every completion of the training is cause for celebration: Tabra employees receive a certificate, a rose, and lots of applause at a staff meeting to acknowledge their accomplishments.

IV

"You have to always keep your priorities straight, and if push came to shove, I'd be in front of a customer before a banker or an analyst any day. But they are a legitimate constituency and principal stakeholders in your success. You need to service them, just as you do major customers."

HARVEY JONES
CEO of Synopsys,
a public company
in Mountain View, Calif.

155
IDEA

Accounting for Bankers

Even when your company is just starting out, you have a right to expect your financial advisers to help make connections for you. For instance, **accountants should be good sources for banking contacts**, and if you're in the market for both, you should make sure that your potential accountant can help deliver entries to bankers as well.

Flo Gillen remembers that when Soft Inc., her computer-programming consulting firm, was just a five-person operation, it was growing rapidly and needed a credit line fast. So when she interviewed potential accountants, Gillen asked point-blank what kind of banking connections their firms could provide on top of their regular accounting services. All but one, it turned out, were vague in their answers; the other accountant, says Gillen, "was pretty blatant about it" and offered introductions to bankers he knew at Chase, Chemical, and Citicorp. That made the difference, and soon Gillen had not just an accountant but credit lines to choose from.

"Sure it was gutsy, but we needed the money, and it worked," says Gillen. Today, her New York City company employs more than 50 programmers.

Tell-All Books Win All Bankers

Most business owners insist that bankers don't understand the financial realities of growing a company. Bankers retort that business owners are out of touch with the reality of credit rules and banking regulations.

Jo Anne Schiller, chief executive of Everyday Learning, a $7-million educational publisher, in Evanston, Ill., thinks she has no choice but to let her banker know everything about her business. "Our financial picture is very complicated because our business is seasonal: 85% of our orders come in from May to September. We couldn't survive without a bank line of credit."

When her bankers asked for as much information as she could give them, she **responded with an annual forecast "full of excruciating detail."** In the 12-page document, Schiller includes best- and worst-case forecasts of how many sales units will move and how many dollars they'll bring in. At every step along the way, she spells out the assumptions behind the numbers.

The unusual degree of disclosure has built up her credibility with her bank. That's made it easier, says Schiller, to get and keep the credit she needs.

157 IDEA

Finding Free Checking

I t may not seem like it sometimes, but many banks are going to greater lengths to keep small-business customers happy. Sometimes it's just a matter of noticing where the costs are adding up and asking the bank for advice.

That tactic worked for Randy Rolston, CEO of Victorian Papers, a $5-million mail-order catalog and two-time *Inc.* 500 company, in Kansas City, Mo. When Rolston told his banker he was being eaten alive by the 12¢ to 20¢ handling charges on each of the 300 to 400 checks his business was processing daily, his bank suggested **a money-market account that lets him process checks for free**. Rolston made the change and has been saving from $60 to $70 a day.

Keeping Tabs on Your Bank

As if you don't have enough to worry about, here's something else: business owners—some of whom have been burned—recommend you keep at least nominal track of the health of your bank.

Chastened by a rampant savings-and-loan crisis in his state, Gary Salomon, CEO of American Fastsigns, in Dallas, makes a habit of monitoring the financial performance of the banks where he does business. The effort has paid off: Salomon got out of one former bank four months before it went belly up.

Business-insurance broker Fred Armstrong wasn't so lucky. One morning in 1994 he opened up the newspaper to find that one of his banks was under a cease-and-desist order, even though it showed an operating profit. Armstrong now **tracks the performance of his banks with two bank-rating services** and switches whenever the banks fail to get high marks.

And Terry MacRae, cofounder and president of Hornblower Dining Yachts, in San Francisco, meets regularly with everyone from his loan officer to the bank president. Each quarter the bankers get to see what their loans are buying, and MacRae gets to check out what bank management changes are underfoot and how their short- and long-term plans are coming along. "When you ask what's new," says MacRae, "it's surprising what they'll tell you."

Don't be afraid, he urges, to turn the tables and make requests of your bank. "They're selling a service, and you're paying for it. You have a right to ask for certain things without being bashful."

1<u>59</u>
IDEA

BANKING

Rebounding from Rejection

If you get a thumbs down from a bank for financing, don't just skulk away. As with most rejections, it presents an opportunity for helpful feedback. Wait a day or two, then **phone the banker to ask for a face-to-face meeting**. George M. Dawson, a veteran banker and now consultant, in San Antonio, Tex., says that if you assure the lender you're not trying to change his or her mind and that you respect the bank's decision, the chances for getting a meeting are "a little better than even."

Once there, ask lots of questions. "Your goal is to learn what steps you need to take to make your company creditworthy," says Dawson. "The best way is to learn all you can about the weakness the bank sees in either your company or the presentation." Be calm and don't be critical, "even if it takes extra patience and self-control." And ask for advice. If the banker can tell you how to rework your business plan or offer specific suggestions (e.g., lease a machine rather than buy it), you'll improve your chances on the next go-round.

160 IDEA

• MANAGING MONEY •

BANKING

Borrowing from Microlenders

When Wee Tai Hom was in search of a $2,000 to $3,000 loan to expand his year-old aquaculture market and art gallery, AquaSource, in the Soho section of New York City, he was roundly turned down by four banks. His problem: he lacked a track record. Not only that, but he was running a start-up company in a start-up industry.

His solution: **forget the banks, and try a microenterprise lender**. These businesses act as intermediaries between the traditional banking world and entrepreneurs, borrowing money from banks and then lending it to individuals. In 1995, there were some 250 microenterprise lenders in 45 states, which had lent out more than $44 million in the previous five years.

Hom secured a $1,000 loan from microlender Accion International three weeks after he applied. "They looked at my business but really focused on the credibility of the person," he says. The loan enabled Hom to establish a credit history "far sooner than I'd otherwise have been able. It expedited that process by two to three years." What's more, each time Hom repays an Accion loan on time, he's eligible to apply for a larger one. (Accion has lent close to $2 million to 488 companies.)

To order an inexpensive directory of microenterprise lenders, call the Aspen Institute, in Queenstown, Md. (410-820-5326). The U.S. Small Business Administration's Answer Desk (800-827-5722) also offers information about microloan programs.

161
IDEA

BANKING

Making Your Image More Professional

Having a hard time getting bankers to understand your business? Let a trade magazine do some of the explaining for you. When Mark Winward was CEO of Jane Ink and in the business of silk screening and embroidering T-shirts, "all bankers could think of was sex, drugs, and rock and roll, while I was trying to get them to think of Boeing golf shirts." **Sending subscriptions of trade magazines to current and prospective bankers**, he says, gave credibility to his appeal that his young company's financials couldn't. That credibility paid off: when Winward's Seattle company was doing $3.5 million in sales, it boasted a $500,000 line of credit.

What If Your Bank Folds?

When a bank goes belly up, Federal Deposit Insurance Corporation (FDIC) insurance protects a depositor's first $100,000 (which is why it's best to use several banks if you're keeping more than $100,000 in bank accounts). But if you've borrowed money from a bank, be aware that **your fate if the bank goes bankrupt will be tied to your repayment performance**. If you've stayed current on your loans, the original loan agreements remain in effect whether those assets are purchased by another bank or managed by the FDIC itself. So from a cash-flow standpoint, there will be no risk.

Delinquent borrowers, on the other hand, will run into trouble. If you've gotten behind on payments and your bank closes its doors, you'll have to work out a payment schedule that puts payments on a current basis. The FDIC has the power to ask for new collateral or additional cosigners. In short, no borrower is off the hook when a bank goes out of business—but only good customers can expect little to change.

REAL WORLD

"Each time you decide to grow again, you realize you're starting at the bottom of another ladder. When we went from one to two stores, we had to commit to getting a refrigerated truck. We could have stopped at two stores and made a nice living, but we decided to move into the central baking plant and take on a tremendous overhead. We wanted to bring on a chief financial officer, and MIS and accounting people, and each time you do that you make a commitment to grow the company a little more."

KEN ROSENTHAL
founder of Saint Louis Bread Co.,
a cafe chain based in St. Louis

163 IDEA

Barter to Keep Your Cash

Bill Martin, the president and owner of U.S. Fitness Products, a $1.5-million retailer of fitness equipment, in Raleigh, N.C., has relied on **barter arrangements to protect corporate cash flow** since 1992. "I joined a local chapter of BXI, an international bartering network, for just a few hundred dollars," says Martin, "and since then I consider the pros and cons of bartering before I make any business decision."

BXI members earn barter "dollars" by swapping their own goods and services for credit toward the purchase of goods and services from other members. When Martin's company relocated, he paid for all the carpentry, electrical work, lighting systems, plumbing, and office furniture through barter dollars, which saved him from having to lay out between $20,000 and $30,000 in cash.

Barter, though, requires prudence. "Sometimes I have to slow down and limit my barter sales and purchases," says Martin. "After all, I still have to meet payroll and pay our rent, utility, and other bills with cash." Remember, too, that the larger the barter network you join, the more chances you'll have to work out the trades that you'll need. Also remember that as far as the Internal Revenue Service is concerned, anything you trade should be reported as income.

164
IDEA

CASH FLOW

Putting Your Start-up on Plastic

When Karen Behnke launched her San Francisco-based company PacifiCare Wellness, in 1983, she financed the start-up with 17 credit cards. "If you open them all on the same day, they'll all be approved," she notes.

That trick would probably still work today, but if you do turn to credit cards to feed a cash-starved business, be sure to **distinguish corporate charges from personal ones**. One conspicuous way to do it is to use different cards for each. "Your corporate charges may qualify for tax deductions on the interest principal," says Sid Morgenbesser, a partner at M.R. Weiser & Co., a New York City accounting firm. "But without good documentation and a clear separation from your personal purchases, that won't work."

Morgenbesser, however, recommends considering other options like borrowing against life insurance or cashing in an IRA before tapping into credit-card financing. Even with a 10% penalty, cashing in an IRA could end up costing much less than credit cards, which carry annual interest rates topping 18%.

165 IDEA

Surviving a Cash Crunch

Some small-business executives say that when you're strapped for cash, it's best to explain the situation to your suppliers and ask for extensions on your payment schedule. Others, however, recommend that you keep the problem to yourself.

That's what Jim Ansara did when his company, Shawmut Design & Construction, in Boston, was in the hole $550,000. While he worked to solve the core problem of poor financial controls, Ansara kept his vendors and subcontractors in the dark by paying bills in 30 to 35 days, much *faster* than the industry average.

The trick, of course, was coming up with the cash. To do that, he **took only high-margin jobs from customers he knew would pay promptly**. When possible, he completed work ahead of schedule and billed some jobs twice a month. He also convinced a few customers to pay for work up front, in exchange for a discount.

The plan worked so well that suppliers never suspected the company was in trouble, and Ansara had the time he needed to get the company back in the black.

166
IDEA

COLLECTIONS

Hedge Against Currency Hazards

If you do business internationally, take steps to protect your international accounts receivable against currency fluctuations.

William Zink, an international tax partner at the Chicago office of the accounting firm Grant Thornton, says that "the first rule of thumb is to **get your international receivables denominated in dollars**. That way, your foreign customers assume the currency risk." Many U.S. companies, he adds, are afraid to ask their customers to agree to this, but you should try. "They're often much more willing to agree than you might expect," says Zink.

If they won't, Zink encourages companies to "enter into simple hedging contracts that will protect you against currency swings that occur during your typical collection period, whether that is 30, 60, or 90 days." For a fee that is usually about 1%, hedging—where you pay to reduce the risks of investment loss—"builds in stability while allowing you to eliminate the prospect of currency-generated losses," says Zink. It also saves you from being taxed on those short-term gains: since 1986, the IRS has been authorized to assess taxes on the "fictional income" that results from foreign-currency swings.

167
IDEA

Time Out for Foreign Cash Flow

Art Allen founded Allen Systems, a manufacturer of mainframe-computer software, with $2,000 from personal savings in 1986. By 1993, the company had grown to $12.5 million in sales. Allen credits the company's growth, in large part, to his obsessive focus on daily cash management.

"With $3 million worth of receivables—about half of that being paid by international customers into our overseas bank accounts—we could not afford to tie up our cash while we waited to act on weekly or monthly bank statements," Allen says.

Instead, by 2 p.m. each day, an accounting staffer at Allen's Naples, Fla., headquarters **receives faxes updating the status of each of the company's international bank accounts**—total deposits, the U.S. exchange rate, and a current value in U.S. dollars of the company's checking and money-market accounts. (The company set up the overseas bank accounts to deposit overseas collections faster.) Each day, Allen decides how much cash should stay in the foreign banks and how much should be transferred back to the United States. "To get money back here from a bank in Brazil or Spain might take two weeks or more," he explains.

TECH
TIP

The cost of such intensive cash management is about $1 per day for each bank's fax and an hour of a staff person's time. Allen spends only 10 minutes a day making his decisions, and the results, he says, "are well worth it."

168 IDEA

COLLECTIONS

International Credit Checks

How do you check the credit ratings of customers and suppliers in foreign countries? As a first step, "take advantage of connections with your bank," advises Richard Worth, CEO of R.W. Frookies, a cookie manufacturer, in Sag Harbor, N.Y. Your bank should have access to **information on foreign companies' credit**, especially if it has branches or affiliations overseas. If not, maybe it's time for a bigger bank.

Within 30 to 60 days it can provide you with *World Traders Data Reports*, which are available for companies in most countries. A one-page report costs about $100 and includes contact information, annual sales, and an assessment of the company's overall financial status. The reports are compiled from research provided by private firms and embassy staff members.

An additional option is to require letters of credit from customers. Written by a bank, a letter of credit guarantees the payment of drafts up to a specified amount within a specified time limit. Essentially, it transfers risk to the bank. But you pay for transaction costs and for every amendment to the deal.

Slashing Shipping Errors

Most business problems can be alleviated by setting measurable goals for improvement, with rewards for achieving them. That was the case at Trelltex, an industrial rubber products wholesaler, in Houston, that wanted to trim its shipping errors.

The $6-million company set up a challenge. To emphasize how important solving the shipping problem was for its growth, **the company offered employees bonuses for low numbers of shipping errors**—the lower the number, the bigger the bonus. It also instituted a "No Surprises Guarantee Program" for customers, promising to ship goods within 24 hours, notify customers of back-ordered items prior to shipping, ship the correct goods, and make no pricing errors. "If we fail you in these areas," stated the written pledge, "we will mail you a check for $25 to help compensate for the inconvenience of our error."

Trelltex set aside $250 a month to cover the guarantee and promised its order-handling staffers that whatever was not spent each month to compensate customers would be passed out to them in cash. The result? CEO Ed Lake says that the company went from making 10 shipping errors a month—at an estimated cost of about $200 apiece—to just two or three. "It has saved us a fortune," says Lake.

170
IDEA

COST CONTROL

Name That Value

Sometimes the first step to controlling costs is making sure people actually know *what* things cost. When Sundance Spas, a Chino, Calif., plastic hot-tub maker, launched a one-year program to reduce its cost of goods, it began with a **companywide session of "The Price Is Right."**

"The game taught purchasing agents in a few minutes why it's important to tell people the value of things," says CEO Ron Clark. In one instance, employees guessed that a plastic part frequently broken during manufacture cost only $2 and then discovered that its actual price was $32.40. Almost across the board, Sundance employees were surprised by how much they'd underestimated costs. Many of them went on to offer ideas for savings. "Just six weeks after they learned that," says Clark, "the production people came up with a two-piece design for the part. Now, when the piece has to be replaced, it costs us $2 rather than $32.40."

Sundance's revenues now top $35 million, and it employs about 250 people. "If you've got to do some belt tightening, I think the game is an effective way to break the news," says Clark.

171
IDEA

The Profit-Promoting Daily Scorecard

Ted Castle was a hockey coach at the University of Vermont before he founded Rhino Foods, a Burlington, Vt., specialty-bakery foods manufacturer. So it's only logical that, like other companies dotting the country, he would figure out a way to **turn business into a game, with rules, strategies, and prizes**.

"The opponent here is expenses," says Castle. To get employees to understand and keep aware of costs, at noon each day, the previous day's "results" are posted near the entrance to Rhino's production room. A daily scorecard lists detailed information including the cost of goods produced, operating expenses, net profit after taxes, and, at the bottom, what the day's bonus is.

Daily information is key, says Castle. "If we have any production problems, they show up on the scorecard the very next day. People see it in plenty of time to make a difference." If the company makes at least 6% net profit at the end of the four-week stretch, each employee gets a bonus check. "For most businesses, it takes a whole year to go from beginning to end," says Castle. "How many people like to play a game that lasts all year long?"

The game succeeded where pep talks alone failed: Rhino's employment has nearly tripled to 58, while revenues and profits have grown by about 600%.

172 IDEA

COST CONTROL

Bag the Bags

L ittle things can add up to big savings. Take packing materials. Sun Sportswear, in Kent, Wash., used to ship its T-shirts in plastic poly-bags. But, in 1990, the company decided that the bags were overkill—costly to the business and harmful to the environment.

When the $73-million company started shipping its shirts, tank tops, and sweats right in the box, **the new packing method** had an unexpected benefit: the clothes arrived less wrinkled because they didn't slide around as much. Customers, including Wal-Mart, Kmart, and Bradlees, didn't miss the plastic a bit.

As for cost savings, at 5¢ a polybag, Sun wound up saving about $37,500 the first year alone.

173 IDEA

Sharing What You've Customized

O ff-the-shelf software programs often just don't do the trick. A company has to make an investment—either by hiring consultants or by devoting personnel time—in customizing a product. One way to dilute the costs is to **resell the new customized product** to other companies with the same demands.

That's what Paric Corp., in St. Louis, did when it was a $40-million construction company. Prepackaged software couldn't meet the growing company's specialized demands, so CEO Paul McKee hired contract programmers to set up and continually refine a customized software package for functions including subcontractor bidding and accounting. The finished product, as it turned out, generated interest from other local construction companies. So Paric set up a new division, Paric Computer Solutions, to market the program. With two salespeople and five programmers, the division sold $500,000 worth of software in its first full year alone.

174
IDEA

COST CONTROL

Opting for Open-Book

You can't judge businesspeople by the color of their collars. Like everyone new to the idea of open-book management—the system where all employees know how the business makes money and what they can do to help it—Bill Fotsch had to learn that lesson.

Fotsch is now a business adviser at Springfield Remanufacturing Corp. (SRC), an engine remanufacturing operation that also helps educate other businesses about the **virtues of going open-book**. Not long ago, though, he was vice-president for business development at Case Corp., the giant farm-machinery company. One day he flew down to visit SRC,. in Springfield, Mo., which his boss had described to him as a "small but innovative supplier." Once there, he wanted to find out if SRC employees really knew the business inside and out. So he asked a guy who was polishing crankshaft journals what the price of the crankshaft was.

At Case, thought Fotsch, such a question would probably provoke a grievance for trying to embarrass a union worker. He figured he'd get no answer and that he'd probably wind up explaining the difference between *price* and *cost*. Instead, the SRC employee looked up and asked, "list price or dealer net?" The worker then went on to explain both prices, how they compared with SRC's cost, and what his own component of the cost was. "At that moment," says Fotsch, "I became a convert."

175 IDEA

Controlling Sky-High Costs

It can pay to have someone on staff serve as **an in-house travel agent scouting out bargains**. While working with an outside agency to make the actual travel arrangements, this person can examine the company's travel requirements and suggest bulk deals or employee policies to save costs. Here are some factors to consider:

- You may want to restrict employees' use of the frequent-flyer miles they earn while traveling for business. If you decide the company owns those miles, consider paying employees a portion of the savings those frequent flyer miles generate.
- Double check to make sure that hotels aren't sending bills to both the company and the traveler's personal account.
- For employees traveling toward the end of the week, compare daily car-rental rates with weekend rates, many of which run Thursday through Sunday.

176
IDEA

EQUITY

Reacquiring Your Equity

One of the worst mistakes Bart Breighner believes he's made since founding Artistic Impressions, an art retailer, in Lombard, Ill., was undervaluing the stock he sold to raise early capital.

In the mid-1980s, Breighner sold equity to five private investors. But as the company grew profitable (annual sales are now $33 million), he began regretting what he'd done. "I've offered several hundred thousand dollars to one investor who originally put in $45,000, but she just won't sell," he says.

Granted, the investor, like the other four, took a risk back when the company was losing $140,000 on sales of $650,000. What Breighner wishes he'd done was **structure his equity sale to include a buyback feature** that would have let him reacquire stock at some fixed future date or growth stage. If he could do it over again, his dream deal would include profit guarantees for investors in the event of a stock buyback—perhaps payouts comparable with the 30% rate of annual return targeted in venture-capital deals—if the company reached sales and profit targets. In effect, he wishes he'd structured a loan of equity rather than a sale of equity. Such a plan "might have scared off some potential investors," Breighner says. "But the flip side of that is that once you've given away your stock, it's very tough to get it back."

177
IDEA

Selling Temporary Equity

Patrick Lammert and Mark Weber were 25 years old when they decided to start a business in an industry they both knew—color separation. They had scraped together $50,000 but needed $50,000 more. They found someone who was willing to front them the money—and give them their first business—but he wanted 51% ownership in return. So they cut a deal that allowed the entrepreneurs to own their business entirely themselves later on: all involved in the transaction were keen on arranging a **mandatory buyback of equity five years later**.

Jack Schumann, the investor, was willing, in effect, to lend the venture money if it put up its equity as collateral. He wanted an active role helping the entrepreneurs manage the company properly. Part of the deal, too, was that Lammert and Weber's company, Wisconsin Technicolor, in Pewaukee, would pay Schumann 5% of gross sales each month as a consultant fee. "I think it was a real good benefit for us," says Lammert of having Schumann around. He credits Schumann with giving the company habits like focusing on profitability and designing good work flows for clients.

In 1994, the two founders paid about 9% of the previous year's $3.2 million revenues to Schumann to reacquire the 51% equity. They were happy, but so too was Schumann: his $50,000 investment had grown to $280,000, a 41% compound annual growth rate.

178
IDEA

EQUITY

One Founder, Two Votes

What most founders fear when it's time to raise money is losing control. It's not a groundless fear; many entrepreneurs who sell a majority of their stock to bring in capital are later thrown out by investors when times get tough.

One way around the dilemma is to **retain operational control by establishing a voting trust**. In effect, you sell off financial equity, but retain voting equity—you can own less than 50% of a company but still control the decision making.

Investors may well demand more shares or a lower share price in return for giving up their voting rights, and many may refuse to play at all. But the dilution of share prices is worth it, argues Robert Ronstadt, who raised money for Lord Publishing, in Natick, Mass., this way. "It's imperative that the lead entrepreneur maintains the management control to fulfill his or her vision for the company," he says. "The opportunity for Monday-morning quarterbacking is incredible."

IDEA

Keeping Tabs on Return Yardage

Some may regard it as an exercise in masochism, but after Jerry Jones bought the Dallas Cowboys in 1989—a sports franchise that had lost almost $10 million on revenues of $41 million the year before—he got into the habit of carrying **a 2- by 2 ½-inch "report card"** in his wallet that tells him exactly how his investment is doing financially.

Once a month, Cowboys treasurer Jack Dixon runs a fresh set of numbers. He looks at the income generated so far by the team and the stadium, subtracts the initial investment, adds the tax benefits received, and subtracts the interest paid on borrowed money. That's one column. Then he looks at the cash Jones had in hand at the time of the purchase and assumes a conservative 5% net return, after taxes. That's the other column. He prints it out on an adding-machine receipt and gives it to Jones, who keeps it folded in his money clip. The report card tells Jones exactly what it will take to get him back to where he was before he made the leap into professional sports.

"There is no inner pleasure in winning unless it's done on a sound, prudent basis," Jones says. "There is no inner pleasure. None."

180 IDEA

Inside Memo on Insider Info

When small companies go public, they often find themselves unprepared for the enormous financial and legal risks they face from complex Securities and Exchange Commission regulations. "If the SEC decides that one of your directors or officers has traded on inside information, your company or its management can be held financially liable," says Ralph Sutcliffe, a partner at Kronish, Lieb, Weiner & Hellman, in New York City.

To protect yourself and your company, set up a two-tiered compliance program and appoint your chief financial officer, general counsel, or corporate secretary to supervise it. First, send out a memo to all employees explaining that no one can trade the company's stock based on knowledge that hasn't been disclosed to the public. State clearly that anyone who violates the policy will be dismissed. Second, for officers, directors, and others more likely to possess critical inside information, circulate a document that spells out legal issues and consequences, and require people to check with your company's compliance officer before buying or selling company stock.

Some companies take it even further. Research Frontiers, a light-control-research business that has made two stock offerings, requires all employees, regardless of position, to **meet with the company's general counsel before purchasing stock**. The Woodbury, N.J., company also monitors its employees' stock trades involving company licensees or suppliers.

181 IDEA

Do-It-Yourself Public Offering

Not long ago, most small companies gave scant consideration to selling stock to the public. The time and expense of complying with Securities and Exchange Commission filing requirements and the continuing paperwork for disclosure were too daunting. Moreover, most companies go public with the help of investment bankers, who prefer to underwrite offerings of $10 million or more.

But since 1989, there's been a simplified process for raising up to $1 million on the public market. Called **the small corporate offering registration, or SCOR,** it's designed for finance amateurs who own demonstrably solid companies.

The vehicle worked wonders for Real Goods Trading Corp., a mail-order company, in Ukiah, Calif. Real Goods financed its initial growth by cash flow, but by 1991 needed a chunk of money to expand its infrastructure. CEO John Schaeffer wrote a prospectus himself using a computer program that guided him through the highly formatted SCOR preparation. The outcome: Real Goods had to turn away $350,000 in the first offering and eventually did another round, raising a total of $4.6 million—essentially on its own.

One note of caution: some CEOs report it took them more time than it did Schaeffer to complete the paperwork. And Drew Field, a San Francisco securities lawyer who has written a book on the subject, says it helps to have a ready group of potential investors and a way to get in touch with them, as Real Goods did with its customer mailing list.

182
IDEA

INVESTOR RELATIONS

Financials for Insiders

It's probably safe to assume that most investors know how to read a financial statement, but if the owners of your company are your employees—as is the case with companies owned in part by employee stock ownership plans (ESOP)—you're better off assuming that people could use some help. After all, sharing an income statement and balance sheet can be a powerful tool for motivating performance, but not if people don't understand what they're looking at.

At Reflexite, an employee-owned manufacturer, in Avon, Conn., **financial statements come with annotations for each line item**. The idea came from a discussion that Cecil Ursprung, president and CEO, had with key managers. "One of my bright, capable managers said 'I hope you publish something different from what I got, because I don't know how to read the thing," recalls Ursprung, who figured he had to do some educating if ownership was going to mean anything to employees.

Now, every financial statement that Reflexite employee-owners receive comes with explanations, in the right margin, for each item. For instance, next to "prepaid expenses," it says, "This is the value of expenses paid in advance, such as insurance premiums."

Take Inventory—for Three Years

I f you're buying a company or contemplating a merger, **demand at least three years of audited financials**. Why? Because an audit of a single year won't catch critical trends, such as slow-moving inventory.

William Webster learned that the hard way. Many years ago, he was negotiating to merge his software company with another software business, which was in the middle of its first complete audit. Webster sent his own team of auditors in to observe the checkup, which he thought would be enough. "The audit certainly didn't turn up any great cause for concern," says Webster.

But it didn't show the whole picture. "We later found out that the company had hundreds of thousands of dollars of inventory that simply wasn't salable and would have to be written off," says Webster. Fortunately, he discovered the problem in time to cancel the merger. Three years of information, he thinks, would have helped to identify earlier the material that was mistakenly adding to the value of the company.

184
IDEA

MERGERS

Know What You're Getting Into

Before you invest time or money in pursuing a company that's for sale, find out if the company is *really* for sale. "Maybe the owner just put the business up for sale to test the market, so he or she could sleep better at night knowing that the business is worth a half million dollars," says Susan Pravda, a mergers-and-acquisitions specialist with the Boston law firm Varet Marcus & Fink. "Maybe family members or a spouse put him or her up to it, and when the business does not sell for the asking price, the owner can go back and say, 'See, I tried, but there is no one willing to buy.'"

People who have put their businesses on the block sometimes end up discovering that they can actually make more money by keeping it than by selling it. If a business that's worth $650,000, for example, generates $200,000 a year in cash flow, the seller only has a short-term incentive to sell. That's especially the case when potential buyers offer to pay only a portion of the purchase price in cash and the rest in deferred payments.

"The first question every buyer should ask is, Why is the owner selling the business?" says Pravda. If the seller doesn't have a definitive answer, you could be pursuing a false cause.

1**85**
IDEA

Borrowing from Customers

When Van Strom, president of American Design & Manufacturing, a $2-million advertising-specialty manufacturer, in Seattle, needed to buy a $100,000 embroidery machine, he **financed it through an unconventional source: one of his company's biggest customers**. "We would both benefit," he says. "Increasing our production capacity would increase our ability to service that company's needs."

The customer advanced $30,000 as a down payment for the new machine, with Strom's company paying the rest of the cost in monthly installments. American Design then paid off the $30,000 credit, along with the monthly interest charges, by fulfilling production orders for free. Strom agreed that if the company ever became unable to fulfill the orders, he would pay the customer with cash instead of credit. "The deal was so simple, so clean, so fast," Strom says.

The one glitch, though, was the drain on cash flow. "We failed to anticipate how *much* demand that company would have for our product. Its orders came in so quickly—without cash payments attached, of course—that we had to stretch our other payables to meet payroll," says Strom. If he borrows from a customer again, Strom plans to specify six months as a minimum payback period. That will leave his company enough time to take on cash-producing business, too.

186
IDEA

RAISING CAPITAL

Resources: A Financing Roundup

The entrepreneurial quest for financing has spawned an endless stream of **resources that promise success in raising capital**. Here are three sources that do an excellent job of covering different aspects of the hunt:

- *The Financing Sources Databank* (DataMerge, 800-580-1188, $139 with quarterly updates for $50) - Computerized databank lists about 2,500 financing sources of all varieties. Listings have screened out lenders who charge hefty up-front fees. Operating instructions are simple.
- *The Ernst & Young Guide to Financing for Growth* (John Wiley & Sons, 908-469-4400, $14.95) - This book does a comprehensive job of scanning the finance universe and explaining the pros and cons of the money options.
- *Raising Capital: How to Write a Financing Proposal* (Oasis Press, 800-228-2275, $19.95) - Dry but practical advice on how to present your business.

187
IDEA

Tapping Uncle Sam

When Chris Nowak started Rocky Mountain Motorworks, a mail-order distributor of Volkswagen parts, it never occurred to him that **local economic-development programs** would fuel his company's rapid growth.

In 1990, a government program provided Nowak with salary-matching funds to entice him to hire workers who were leaving other government-sponsored programs. Later, when the company had outgrown its Woodland Park, Colo., headquarters and was thinking about moving to a neighboring town, a local economic-development group helped get the company free land at a new industrial park. "That saved us about $500,000," says Nowak, who got a Small Business Administration loan to help pay for construction and a low-interest fixed loan from the Colorado Housing Finance Authority to cover the rest. The town of Woodland Park also bought Nowak's old building, which provided him with the down payment for the construction costs.

To get such help, says Nowak, "you have to demonstrate to these programs that you're creating jobs and local opportunities." But that wasn't difficult for him. What was difficult was figuring out all the accounting that was involved in the complicated deals. "It's important to have the best accounting assistance you can," says Nowak. "Tax incentives and other kinds of deals can be quite complicated." Without the programs, he says, "we could never have grown to $5 million in sales," which the company hit in 1994.

188 IDEA

RAISING CAPITAL

Paying Investors Royalties

There's a middle ground between giving investors an equity share and treating their money as a straight loan. When Andover Advanced Technologies, a sales and marketing company, in Westford, Mass., was two years old, it garnered a $100,000 investment by promising to **pay investors royalties based on sales**.

For companies like Andover Advanced, royalty arrangements postpone the question of valuation and allow the business to distribute cash based on actual sales, keeping decisions about the future in the hands of management (since royalty investors typically don't get formal management control or seats on boards). Investors, meanwhile, can make decisions based on the near-term prospects of products they can see for themselves.

Andover Advanced promised to pay investors between 8% and 12% of new product sales each month. How long it will make payments is contingent on sales. If things go well, the company gets to stop paying when investors have gotten five times their money back—or three times their initial investment, if the money is paid in the first year. Clearly, president Bruce Twickler admits, this type of money can be expensive. But, he says, "If we're successful, we may not need any additional money. And if we do, we think we'll sell stock at a price that's quite a bit higher than anything we could have obtained" before the royalty deal was done.

REAL
WORLD

"In certain economic ways,
the United States has become a
third-world country. Foreign investors
think in bigger, more flexible terms than
Americans do. The American financial
market barrages entrepreneurs with 'This is
the way we do it. Fill out this form.
Write this prospectus.' Well, we're going to
leave U.S. investors in our dust.
Their rigid attitudes
don't fit with the current
global realities and options."

CHRISTOPHER HARTNETT
CEO of USA Global Link, in Fairfield, Iowa.
Hartnett's company, with revenues of $96 million,
turned to Asian investors after becoming discouraged
with U.S. bankers and venture capitalists

189
IDEA

RAISING CAPITAL

Don't Misread Potential Investors

Sometimes the people you think are shoe-ins as investors don't come through, and sometimes the people you think would never invest sign on with little effort on your part. It's **important not to get overconfident or prematurely discouraged when you're raising money**.

Phillip Wade and Huib Geerlings cofounded a wine-by-mail company, Geerlings & Wade (G&W), in Canton, Mass., and took it public in 1994. When they went out for their road show, they learned that they couldn't trust their gut feelings about potential investors. Here are some excerpts from their diary:

"First stop: Milwaukee. Monday morning, hop into a car for a meeting. Half a dozen companies like us present deals like ours. Guy in the audience yawns and walks out. Our goose is cooked! Later, bored guy buys our stock; others who listened intently don't. Proves you can't read the audience.

"Next Monday. Now home, ought to get easier. It doesn't. Five one-on-ones before lunch, then a big lunch. In Boston, the rule is, land the big Fidelity fund first; then, reassured, others will fall in line. Good sign: Fidelity takes lots of prospectuses. Doesn't buy in the end."

The company ended up doing fine: it sold 1.4 million shares at $8 each. But William Herp, G&W's financial officer, says that "you find out how well you've done only when it comes together on the last day."

RAISING CAPITAL

Keep the Door Ajar

One of the hardest things about tapping venture capitalists is getting in to see them. Business plans arrive on their doorsteps daily, and it can be almost impossible to stay on the minds of people juggling so much information.

It's your job to stay in touch. Some entrepreneurs who have been successful raising VC money **keep files on every financier** who has ever expressed even the vaguest interest in their companies, and they mail regular company updates to those potential money sources. Some CEOs do sporadic mailings whenever there's big news; others do quarterly mailings, listing everything from customer updates and new employees to strategic decisions and new product information.

The same holds true with banks: in the event that you may one day have to change banks, it helps if you send financials to a few select banks you don't do business with. If you have to make the switch, the bank will already be acquainted with your company.

191
IDEA

SELLING THE COMPANY

Skip the One-Man Band

Everybody likes to feel important, but when you're selling your company one of the worst mistakes you can make is to emphasize how essential you are to the business. "If the buyer thinks that the company can't be run without you, it becomes less attractive," points out Stan Sanderson, who's spent much of his career in the mergers and acquisitions business.

That may seem obvious, but Sanderson, now CEO of Jostens Learning Corp., an educational software company, in San Diego, says it's common for owners to undermine their own sales pitches by taking too much credit for a company's successes and by exhibiting too much hands-on control. Often they do it unconsciously—stopping during a plant tour, for example, to instruct employees on some detail of their work. A shrewd buyer, says Sanderson, will lower an offer accordingly. His advice: **downplay your role as CEO** and stress the abilities of the entire staff and management team.

Keeping Key Players in Place

For any owner who has decided to put the business on the block, a crucial issue is how to retain key managers before and after the sale. If important employees decide to leave once it becomes clear that a sale is imminent, an owner has two concerns. In the short term, the value of the company may decrease; in the long term, the exodus may sap the ability of the new owners to run the business.

Management contracts along with a bonus plan can help. Contracts generally last from one to three years, while discretionary bonuses are often structured so that a manager gets a cash bonus when the sale is closed and guaranteed bonuses 12 and 24 months later. If the company buyer subsequently replaces the manager, the buyer would still pay the bonuses covered in the agreement, although not the salary.

The best way to defuse problems is to include all managers in the negotiations, whether they're equity holders or not. "Open communication in a sale can go farther than monetary rewards to ensure that key people remain with the company," notes Orville Mertz, a Milwaukee business broker. And Gary Roelke, a senior vice-president in the Teaneck, N.J., office of Geneva Business Services, adds: "In the end, it may be more important for the *buyer* to establish incentives for managers. That goes a long way in forging an important alliance."

193
IDEA

TAXES

Is It a Loan or a Dividend?

t's not unusual for the owners of privately held companies to borrow money from company coffers, believing the cash is theirs to use without triggering unwanted tax liabilities.

But such shareholder loans are risky. "In the worst-case scenario, the IRS decides that the transaction wasn't a loan, it was a corporate dividend," explains Valerie Robbins, a partner at the Washington, D.C., accounting firm of Beers & Cutler. A dividend payment is taxable to its recipient but provides no tax deduction for the corporation. The second-worst-case scenario is that the IRS decides the loan was really compensation, which then gives the corporation a tax deduction, but means the recipient still owes income and Social Security taxes.

To avoid both tax hits on loans, tax professionals advise taking these four steps:

- Document the loan in writing, with signatures from the recipient and company owner—two signatures if they are the same person.
- Observe every formality that would accompany any other official document, including getting it witnessed and filing it in the company's corporate records.
- Include a clause that specifies an annual interest rate for the loan—preferably at least a point above prime.
- Make the interest payments when they come due.

V

"A budget, or a plan, is the secret to freedom. When you know what you need to do, and how you're actually doing, you're liberated. You can deviate from the plan and still be in control — in fact, the freedom to deviate without losing control is one of the great benefits of having a clear plan in the first place.

"Your plan, which is essentially your profit-and-loss statement, should be so simple you can meditate on it, modify it, adjust it, and correct it while lying awake in the dark at night, driving in a car, leaning back with your eyes closed on an airplane, or keeping yourself occupied during a dull meeting."

KENNETH H. OLSEN
founder and president emeritus
of Digital Equipment Corp., in Maynard, Mass.

194
IDEA

ADVISERS

Know the SCORE

Need advice on planning, marketing, pricing? Many people find informal advisers who help guide them, but there are also formal ways to **hook up with mentors who know the business of business better than you**.

The Service Corps of Retired Executives (SCORE) joins entrepreneurs one-on-one with experienced businesspeople. It also oversees broader programs; for instance, shortly after Richard Rose cofounded a health-food company, he applied for and was chosen to take part in SCORE's Adopt-an-Emerging-Business program. For a year, local experts gave him almost-free guidance in marketing, finance, and management. Sharon's Finest, in Santa Rosa, Calif., is now a $3-million company.

Karen Behnke, whose PacifiCare Wellness, in San Francisco, is now a $6-million business, was chosen in her early years of running the company to take part in a Stanford Business School project. For a year, students helped her write a business plan and investigate the marketplace. The class, she says, helped her think about everything from her competitive advantages to her exit strategy. "It also helped me lose emotional possessiveness," she adds.

1 95
IDEA

Cultivate Mentors from Everyday Contacts

I'm a wimp, and I like the handholding." So says Mary Baechler, head of Racing Strollers, a Yakima, Wash., manufacturer of baby strollers for joggers, of her penchant for using mentors. As she has grown the company and taken on bigger challenges, Baechler has actively **sought out experienced businesspeople who are willing to take on the role of mentor**.

The first was a local businessman recommended by a banker who turned Baechler down for a loan. "That mentor taught me to love my financial statements," says Baechler. The second, she met by cold calling a multinational corporation and asking the chairman's secretary whom the company had worked with to set up international distribution. "I cold called the referral as well, and he told me so much about distribution in our first conversation that I kind of threw myself at him and said, 'Gee, will you teach me?'" The third, she met at a management-education program.

Not only have the tutors walked her through her initial business issues, but they've consistently helped her troubleshoot problems as well. Baechler estimates she spends an average of two to three hours a week on the phone with them, and she will often run important ideas by all three. Sometimes they offer three different alternatives; other times they support the course she's already opted for. "I'm always amazed at the generosity of people who will take the time to teach novices," Baechler adds.

1 96
IDEA

Educated Guesses

If you're like many CEOs, your idea of a good candidate for the board of directors is a no-nonsense executive. That's fine, but to judge by Joe Crugnale's experience, you should **consider business school academics for your board**, too. Professors can bring big-picture perspectives to your management.

In the early years of growing two restaurant chains in New England, Crugnale recruited Bert Mendelsohn, then a professor of marketing at Boston College, who specialized in tracking small food-service chains. Mendelsohn helped Crugnale with the nuts and bolts of understanding an operating statement and determining what ratios he needed to hit to make his restaurants more competitive. Mendelsohn's classes also did market research for Crugnale.

The professor was elected to the board to help plan long-term strategy. His mercilessly logical approach complemented Crugnale's more intuitive approach. Today, Crugnale's pizzeria chain, Bertucci's, headquartered in Wakefield, Mass., is a $103-million business with 67 restaurants.

197 IDEA

Limits on Lawyers

Lawyers make good advisers, but their role should be clarified before they're invited to join the board of directors. The trouble, says Dennis O'Connor, a lawyer with a Waltham, Mass., firm specializing in corporate law, is that things can get confusing when a lawyer is asked to wear two hats—those of business adviser and legal counselor. "There's a gray area in between, and it can be hard for a CEO who acts counter to a lawyer's recommendation to know whether he is risking an illegality or simply disagreeing on business strategy," says O'Connor.

It's standard policy at many law firms to sit on the boards of companies they advise, says O'Connor, because that makes it difficult for clients to sever the relationships. His own firm has a different—and he thinks healthier—approach. O'Connor attends as many as eight board meetings a month, but only as a **non-voting legal adviser**. Businesses get the best of both worlds: legal advice, without the confusion of wondering in whose interest the advice is given.

"Many companies try to save money by not having a lawyer present at all," says O'Connor, "but that can hold up a decision when a director wheels around and says 'Let's see what the lawyer has to say about this.'"

198
IDEA

BOARDS

Committing to Your Board

If you're going to have a company board—formal or informal, with liability or not—you must **commit to spending time regularly on board-related matters**. Without at least a 10% time commitment, says Ray McCormick Jr., CEO of American Sweeteners, a $9-million company, in Frazer, Pa., "you won't get the right people, and you won't get them involved in running your business."

McCormick, who has had several different boards during his company's lengthy history, set up an advisory council to help make decisions on issues such as acquisitions. Council members were identified through third-party introductions and then interviewed twice by McCormick. They attend four meetings a year at company headquarters and meet with McCormick individually between sessions.

Perhaps the most time-consuming part of the process, says McCormick, is deciding which issues should be placed on the council's quarterly agendas and then compiling backup reports on those items for the board. But it's all necessary—and useful. "What we're really talking about is running the company," says McCormick, adding that the responsibilities don't take time away from managing so much as hone his own options.

Focusing on the Big Picture

The biggest problem with strategic goals is that most of the time they're communicated to employees just once —if at all—at the beginning of the year. After that, it's easy to forget that everything everyone does ought somehow to fit into the plan.

However, at Globe Metallurgical, in Cleveland, the 30 managers of the 300-employee, $50-million-plus company stay on track by using a master calendar that not only shows which team members are working on what, but also **shows how those jobs relate to the company's strategic goals**.

It works like this: The company, which produces metal alloys and has 300 employees, developed a five-year plan for improving quality and cutting costs. The plan consisted of a 20-page list of nearly 100 numbered items. Using a daily calendar, the company lists, in shorthand, who's doing what and which number on the list that work corresponds to. So one day's entry might read, "#56 - Curt Goins, visit Union Carbide, perform supplier quality audit." Managers keep copies of the 20-page list for more details and deadlines for each item.

"It's not so much a matter of accountability as what we need to do and when," says Goins, who was director of quality at the time the list was developed. "The calendar prods you." Measures like this helped Globe win a Malcolm Baldrige National Quality Award.

200 IDEA

COMMUNICATION

'To Do' Lists Keep Team in Touch

As companies grow, it's difficult to keep up with what everyone's doing. Opportunities for teamwork often get lost. Norman Howe, CEO of Norman Howe & Associates, a marketing and consulting business, in Pasadena, Calif., says that **shared weekly "to do" lists** are one way to combat inefficiencies.

Every Monday morning, Howe's 26 employees make lists of their tasks or projects. The lists are then shared with supervisors and read at a staff lunch. A big advantage of operating this way, Howe says, is the team atmosphere it creates. "People have a more complete view of what's happening," he says, "and there's a real value in articulating what you're working on to a group." During the staff lunches, which usually last about an hour, individuals frequently suggest new ways to approach problems. If they have time, they often offer to help colleagues in a pinch.

REAL
WORLD

"Getting to check
something off your list is
like getting morphine,
literally. It's been
scientifically proven that
checking things off lists
releases endorphins in
your body."

HYRUM SMITH
founder of Franklin International Institute,
in Salt Lake City,
maker of the Franklin Day Planner

201 IDEA

EDUCATION

Share-and-Tell

The best way to make education dollars go further is to **ask employees to share what they learn with their colleagues**.

When employees of Linda L. Miles & Associates, a seminar company for health-care professionals, in Virginia Beach, Va., return from attending a seminar or conference, they give a short presentation of the three most important things they learned. It's a great way to get people to follow up, says CEO Linda Miles. It can also give people greater empathy toward those in other jobs. "After our shipping clerk went to a postal-service seminar," reports Miles, "employees learned how complex his job was and were more cooperative."

At Davis, Hays & Co., in Maywood, N.J., employees give book reports once a month. "We don't assign books," says president Alison Davis, although the public-relations firm does pay for them. "It just has to be related somehow to our business." Employees talk about what the book— or video, or book-on-tape—is about, what is interesting in it, and what they learned that could help the company. There's an added benefit, too. Since presenters go before the group and use overhead projectors and charts, it helps people develop presentation skills.

Tests to Inspire Learning

Remember back in school when you'd cram before a big test? Sometimes **having those tests was the only way to force yourself to learn** the material. The same holds true in the workplace.

When Diesel Technology Corp. (DTC), in Wyoming, Mich., wanted to make sure employees knew the assembly process for the more than 40,000 fuel injectors it puts together each month, it designed a contest. Every employee of the $81-million business appears before the quality team and is asked to identify each component part, explain its function, and assemble an injector. Successful DTC employees get an "I Got It Together" T-shirt.

Most of the people already knew the material anyway, but those who didn't learned. Within three weeks, 75% of employees had earned their shirt.

203
IDEA

EDUCATION

How to Pick a Seminar

Seminars can be a good way to obtain a broad array of information, but if you need know-how in a particular area, try this: **go to the seminars where the experts teach the pros in their special field**. The experts aren't trying to sell anything, their presentations are more sophisticated, and you can make great contacts in the process.

When Cecil Ursprung, president and CEO of Reflexite, in Avon, Conn., wanted information on employee stock-ownership plans (ESOPs), he attended a seminar for accountants and lawyers who administer ESOPs. "We went to hear the experts whom professionals rely upon," Ursprung says. "The information was presented in an unbiased manner, and they discussed the positives and negatives. We were much better prepared to evaluate our own lawyer's and accountant's advice." And when Reflexite's board voted to set up an ESOP, Ursprung had in hand a list of the best advisers to hire for the transition.

The ESOP program was a success. In 1992, the employees-turned-owners of Reflexite were designated *Inc.*'s Entrepreneurs of the Year.

Calculating Travel Payoffs

What you get out of a business trip usually depends on what you go looking for. If you don't want to miss the big hits, you have to be willing not to be distracted by things that aren't on your agenda.

For Jimmy Calano, cofounder and CEO of CareerTrack, an $80-million, 450-employee seminar company, that means putting a dollar value on his search. "If I'm going to a seminar or a conference, in my mind I'm looking for a **$10,000 idea per day**, whether it's in cost savings or revenue generation," he says. He applies the same kind of criteria when making a decision about whether to travel from his corporate office, in Boulder, Colo., to see a potential client. "If I'm making a sales presentation, the piece of business has to produce $100,000 or more. I know the value of my time—every year I try to calculate that value because it helps me evaluate how I spend it."

To make the most of trips away from the office, Calano also tries to leverage them. He keeps lists by city of people he knows, so that he can quickly check if there's someone he wants to fit in while he's visiting the area.

Info Gathering as Reflex

T he role of managers is to **make sure there's a flood of information coming into the company**," says Bruce W. Woolpert, CEO of Granite Rock, a $100-million company that produces and sells crushed quarry stone, in Watsonville, Calif.

Granite Rock, which in 1992 was one of five companies to win the prestigious Malcolm Baldrige National Quality Award, is known for its customer "report cards," annual surveys that ask buyers to rate the company against its competitors. In addition, the company conducts longer surveys every three or four years to gather more detailed information about customer needs and wants. Focus groups and quick-response cards let the company probe for ideas about new products and services throughout the year.

That's where the big ideas come from. One year, customers at a focus group said that what they really wanted was to be able to pick up rock at any time of the day or night and to get in and out quickly. Those requests led to one of the company's biggest technological innovations: a loading zone dubbed Granite Xpress. Today truckers pick up their crushed stone by pulling up, checking their order on a computer, sticking a magnetic card in a slot, and loading from automatic overhead bins. The system serves the requests articulated at the focus group: it functions around the clock and has cut the time truckers spend at the site from an average of 30 minutes to 10 minutes.

REAL WORLD

"Seymour Cray was a friend of
my dad's. I once asked my dad
what it was like to know the
genius who had built
the world's first supercomputer
company. My dad said,
`Well, actually, son, he wasn't
so much smarter than me.
He just made mistakes a
hundred times faster.'"

TOWNES DUNCAN
chairman and CEO of Comptronix,
in Guntersville, Ala.

206
IDEA

IDEAS

Create a Personalized 'Textbook'

For ideas about day-to-day operations, skimming over a helpful article or book can be like calling on a trusted friend or adviser—the written word can spark ways of thinking about specific needs. Steve Jonak has crafted a system that's simple and low tech and, he says, ensures he's got ideas when he needs them. He's building **a master file of articles categorized by management topic**.

"There's a lot of information out there, and sometimes I don't even have time to absorb the article when I find it," says Jonak, who owns Industrial Steel, a steel service center, in Columbia Heights, Minn. When he comes across an article that seems as if it could be useful in the future, he clips it and files it in an 18-inch box in his office—dubbed his "Run the Company" box—under topics such as Keeping Customers, Delegation, and Safety.

"When you're working on a specific project," says Jonak, "it's nice to be able to pull a whole bunch of articles and have the information right there." It's timesaving because he doesn't have to flip back through books or magazines to find the article he remembers seeing. Jonak also keeps two special files for weekly reading and daily browsing—"motivational stuff"—that helps him, he says, "keep on track."

207 IDEA

Learning from Public Companies

Companies that have gone public and opened themselves to scrutiny by the world can be great sources of free information. Timothy DeMello, CEO of SkyRock, in Newton, Mass., and a former stockbroker, says he **reads every new offering prospectus** he can get his hands on. "I read offerings for companies such as the Franklin Mint—and you think, What does a company that sells Rhett Butler dolls have to do with me? But it's a direct marketer of products and might have ideas about listening to customers or using software-support systems." His best ideas, DeMello says, often come from sources that appear irrelevant.

Other CEOs buy stock in public competitors to get the information those companies regularly generate about the state of the industry, their approach to the marketplace, litigation they're facing, how much they pay their executives, what their cost of goods is, who their suppliers are, and what kind of margins they've been getting. Even without buying stock, prospectuses are available for the asking just by calling the investor relations department of a business.

"I don't believe
in business plans. If you
have a plan, it means
you're not prepared
for change."

BRENDA FRENCH
CEO of French Rags,
in West Los Angeles

IDEAS

The High-Tech Suggestion Box

Companies in which most employees work at networked computers can take advantage of the link to create an updated version of the old suggestion box. The new version: an **online suggestion database**.

At Timeslips, a software publisher, in Essex, Mass., CEO Mitchell Russo says a companywide suggestion database—that anyone can put a suggestion into or peruse—"probably has more than a thousand suggestions in it." The ideas come from customers, letters, developers, and staff. Ranging from fleeting thoughts to formal ideas about product enhancements, the entries each include the idea, who originated it, and the date of the suggestion.

Russo reads through the collection every week or so. "Fifteen to 20 of the items are what I consider great ideas," he says, "and they end up on a short list in my personal database." They also show up in product updates: Russo says that more than 100 electronic-suggestion-box entries were incorporated into one release, and he has overseen development of new products that bubbled up through the idea-exchange system.

IDEAS

Personalized Wisdom

The problem with new books is that they keep you from returning to old ones. You can get so busy trying to keep up with what is coming out that you can forget what you've already read. And it's hard to convince yourself to go back and re-read 300 pages.

One trick: **create your own summaries when you finish reading a book you like**. Underline passages as you read, and type up or photocopy those sections. You'll get a summary that's personalized to your needs and your business. It's easy to go back and re-read it, and you can also share the outlines with other people in your company. They may not read 300 pages, but they'll certainly read your 10.

210 IDEA

Putting Internet Access to Work

You've heard the Internet hype. But what do ordinary businesses *do* with an Internet connection?

Greenville Tool & Die (GTD), a 49-year-old automotive supplier, in Greenville, Mich., **uses the Internet as a source of free software and technical information**. In 1992, John Latva, GTD's systems manager, set up an Internet connection for the company, at a cost of $50 a month plus $7 for each hour online. Latva thought the company would use it just for electronic mail while testing new computer-aided-design (CAD) software: GTD employees wanted to talk with the software's publisher by E-mail rather than use overnight mail.

But soon Latva and a colleague began exploring and came upon a CAD mailing list, through which 250 CAD users at companies such as Fiat and Ford exchange mail about design and software problems. It's been better than getting news from the software manufacturer, Latva says, "because it's up-to-date information from other users." He also discovered a world of free software online and was able to download a program that displays CAD file drawings as if they were completed parts; another free program allows the sales department to run a computer slide show that previews finished dies for customers.

2111
IDEA

Safety Rules the Agenda

The topics you choose to address at meetings say more about your concerns than any posters or memos, particularly with major issues like cost consciousness, profitability, quality, and safety.

In fact, says Gordon Lankton, chairman and president of Nypro, a plastic-injection-molding factory, in Clinton, Mass., you can begin to make your manufacturing operation safer just by **making safety and precaution a constant topic for discussion**. At every meeting at Nypro, whether among the board of directors or the warehouse shipping crew, the first topic is always safety.

The issues range from how to drive a forklift and stack pallets to developing a boot that won't slip on the clean-room floor. When an accident does occur, it's discussed in detail. Even the company's annual banquet begins with a year-to-year comparison of time lost to job-related accidents.

With this emphasis, Nypro's safety performance has been transformed from substandard to award winning. The annual accident rate now hovers between 1 and 2 per 100 employees, which was good enough to warrant an award from the National Safety Council. And healthier employees have contributed to a healthier bottom line; the company's workers' compensation bill fell from a peak of almost $500,000 per year to $100,000.

Tame the Open-Meeting Beast

Busy people resent few things more than having to attend a meeting with an open agenda—or, just as bad, a nebulous one. **The best meetings have a clear focus, a distinct purpose, and a time limit**. They also have agendas that are circulated in advance to everyone attending.

Frederick DeJohn, a director at the Western New York Technology Development Center, in Amherst, N.Y., puts together groups of companies for on-site visits and discussions. He says that making sure host companies prepare adequately is a crucial part of his job. "Once the meeting is under way, it's under way—to jump in would be like trying to stop the *Queen Mary*. The biggest problem is time: people get so wrapped up in what they're saying that they don't want to stop."

To keep the meetings efficient and prevent people from getting sidetracked, DeJohn advises hosts to set time limits for each area of discussion. All attendees are sent or faxed a schedule in advance, so they can prepare their thoughts and have a feel for how the meeting will be paced. Right before the meeting, DeJohn reminds people that they will be sticking diligently to the schedule. "In some sessions we have timekeepers, who will clink a glass when there are two minutes left for each section."

2 1 3
IDEA

MEETINGS

Free Time Is Fruitful Time

I f you're planning a company retreat, don't make the mistake of scheduling meetings from dawn to dusk in a misguided attempt to justify the expense of the time away from the office. You'll get just as much accomplished, and maybe more, if you **let people have free time at the beach or on the golf course**. "When people get together, they always wind up talking about the things they have in common," says one former *Fortune* 500 exec. "What your people have in common is your company, and that's what they're going to discuss, even if they're playing cards. They'll talk about what they're working on."

Besides, you're not going to win points by taking people someplace nice and keeping them cooped up in meetings all day. Better to have focused sessions in the morning and leave the afternoons free. You'll not only have a more successful retreat, but you may win some goodwill as well.

Keeping It Brief

It's not easy to keep blowhards from dominating staff meetings, and it can be difficult to muster the diplomacy to muzzle those people. Even without loudmouths in attendance, meetings can run for hours if everyone wants to make a comment. So when it comes to moderating staff gatherings, being cut-and-dry can work out best. When the weekly staff meetings at Reflexite, a $40-million-plus manufacturer of reflective plastic products, in Avon, Conn., first blossomed from 6 to 14 people, that's what president Cecil Ursprung had to do.

"We realized that if everybody contributed at the same rate as when six people attended, the meeting would last half a day," says Ursprung. His two goals were to allow everyone time to talk and to keep the meeting to an hour and a half. So he **invested in a $6 alarm clock**.

Each staffer gets to stump for six minutes before the alarm rings. "The return on investment is incalculable," quips Ursprung. Meetings keep to their targeted 90 minutes, and Ursprung doesn't have to play the heavy.

215
IDEA

Retreat for Brainstorming Day

Employees often know the most about how to solve growth-related problems—you just need to give them the opportunity to make suggestions.

One way to do it: **a companywide brainstorming picnic/retreat**. Solar Press, a $63-million company, in Naperville, Ill., shuts down its printing plants, rents a space at a nearby community college, and assembles hundreds of full-time workers for a day of information sharing and brainstorming.

One eight-hour retreat, dubbed Solar Brainstorming Day, was complete with T-shirts, a catered lunch, and a beer party. It was held in July, the company's slow month, so that little production time was lost. Top managers gave short speeches, and president and CEO Frank Hudetz presented a slide show on Solar's projected growth and future plans. Employees then met in departmental groups to discuss production bottlenecks, space and equipment needs, and staffing requirements. The upshot: a list of 50 problem areas, each one assigned to an employee task force.

IDEA 216

Annual One-Page Game Plan

Elyria Foundry was losing $3 million a year on revenues of $4 million when Gregg Foster purchased it in 1983. As the company got back on track, Foster began outlining for employees the business's revenues and profits, the new bonus pool, and improvements in attendance and scrap reduction. Looking for a way to focus people even more, he figured he had to give them information about the future, not just the past. So the managers at the metal-castings company, in Elyria, Ohio, began drawing up **a one-page list of the company's goals for the coming year**.

The process starts in November. Managers take suggestions from their departments and submit 5 to 10 goals to Foster, who incorporates items ranging from "build small casting capabilities" to "99% attendance" onto a single list. At the annual meeting in December, he then explains what the company will be shooting for in the coming year.

"I started the goals as an excuse to measure our performance for the annual meeting," says Foster. "I wanted to be able to put up on the overhead projector a list that would light competitive fires." Short and succinct is the rule; most strategic plans, says Foster, are "usually so ethereal that they don't make sense." He also looks for measurable, particular goals. "They're specific, but they also create a picture of how we want to be. They give us things to talk about."

217
IDEA

Plot Out Cash Flow

T he biggest challenge for any young company is "making sure that you have enough capital to begin with and that it will last long enough to determine whether or not the business is viable," says Norm Brodsky, CEO of CitiPostal, in Brooklyn, N.Y. The best way to get your business to the point where it can survive without outside capital is to write a business plan, which Brodsky terms "essentially your best guess as to how you're going to get there."

Basic is better. "I don't mean anything elaborate," says Brodsky. "What I'm talking about is **a modified, down-and-dirty income statement and cash-flow statement**, real simple. A reasonable expectation of sales by month for a year." Writing a detailed month-by-month plan, he says, makes you figure out exactly what you're expecting to sell per day.

When Brodsky helped advise a pair of entrepreneurial novices on their first venture, he said to them, "Let's take July. What can you do in July?" The couple planned to sell $20,000 worth of product, and Brodsky pointed out that with 20 working days in a month, "that's $1,000 per day. An average order is $40, so you're talking about 25 orders a day, three orders an hour, an order every 20 minutes. For a whole month. Can you do it?" The goal of the exercise, Brodsky emphasizes, is not to dampen enthusiasm. For that couple, he says, the answer was "maybe yes, maybe no. The point was to make sure they were dealing with reality."

VI

"When you're growing a business, there are so many things that can attract you to the left or right. People who want to license your products so they can sell them in Venezuela, or people who want you to sell their stuff just because your store is there. Focus is important in managing a business and in influencing customers' response to a business."

ROBERT NOURSE
ex-venture capitalist and CEO
of the Bombay Company, based in Fort Worth, Tex.
Nourse was *Inc.*'s 1993 Entrepreneur of the Year

218
IDEA

ALLIANCES

The Value of Being Precise

It may seem inconvenient or expensive to put agreements with suppliers into precise contracts, but do it anyway. **Vague contracts can come back to haunt you** and plunge your company into legal hassles down the road. They can also reduce the value of your business if you decide to sell.

One lawyer who has handled acquisitions evaluation for a large corporation says that many deals end up being killed because the acquiree had vague contracts. Even if the deal can be saved, he points out, "it costs money to clean things up," and that gets reflected in the acquirer's final valuation.

Common problems include oral agreements that have never been put in writing; lack of a termination date for arrangements; unspecified commitments to provide services for a product; and failure to specify what happens if the contract is breached. If you think you can't afford the legal expense of drafting every agreement, at least have a lawyer develop boilerplate contracts for you.

219
IDEA

ALLIANCES

Getting the Inside Track

Nobody likes to lose a good employee, but sooner or later some of your best people are going to outgrow your company. The danger is that they may leave for one of your competitors. A good alternative is to **be proactive and try to get them better jobs with your vendors**.

That's what Judson Beamsley did when he was running Tek-Aids Industries, a distributor of microcomputer products, in Arlington Heights, Ill. He encouraged employees to talk openly about their job aspirations. "If someone wanted to leave, I'd give him a recommendation," says Beamsley. During one eight-year stretch, he helped 25 people find new jobs—which is a lot, considering that Tek-Aids was employing only around 40 people. But by placing people with his suppliers, Beamsley built a network of company alumni who could tell him about developments in the market. "If I didn't already know what my competitors were doing, I could find out very quickly," he adds.

220 IDEA

EVALUATING

Audit Sizes Up Potential Vendors

In 1991, Softub, a hot-tub manufacturer, in Chatsworth, Calif., ran into a glitch that almost sank it. The company had subcontracted out the assembly of the motor, pump, and control units for its tubs, and the units were breaking down—in testing and after the tubs were installed in customer homes. The supplier went belly up, and Softub got stuck with $500,000 in repairs and bad dealer relations.

Even though Softub CEO Tom Thornbury had met with the vendor twice and talked with its other customers, those checks hadn't been enough. He decided that if he survived, he'd be more thorough. Today, with about 200 suppliers, Softub uses **a detailed audit form to review potential vendors** and has an audit team visit and grill candidates. With 10 of Softub's 130 employees participating, the audit team gathers information ranging from whether the company has military certification to whether it's working at capacity (50% capacity is cause for concern; Softub wants its suppliers busier). The team also looks for housekeeping details, like whether there are oil slicks around machinery.

"We're recruiting a better breed of supplier," says Thornbury. And vendor turnover has been cut in half—a significant savings, since the evaluation can take months and cost several hundred dollars a day.

EVALUATING

Spotting the Problem Vendor

Even if you have a friendly relationship with your supplier, **don't ignore signs of trouble**. Some are fairly obvious, says Douglas A. Phillips, a bankruptcy expert with M.R. Weiser & Co., a New York City-based accounting firm. Phillips cites signals such as the departure of key employees or inexplicable delays in shipments. Other warnings may be more subtle.

Phillips suggests you be on the alert for frequent changes in accountants or lawyers. "If it happens a lot, chances are it's more than a dispute over fees," he says. Also be aware of unexpected sales of assets; if they don't make sense, you should be asking questions. And if your supplier changes its method of financing, say from using a bank line of credit to factoring its receivables, find out more. "It may not mean anything," says Phillips. "Then again, it may be the smoke that leads you to the fire."

Ask for audited financial statements if you're really suspicious. "If you think something's funny and the company doesn't want to provide adequate information," says Phillips, "then you should think twice about the terms you're offering."

FINANCE

The Personal Pay

Sometimes things you do by instinct can have a bigger payoff than you had at first imagined. That was the case for Fred DeLuca, cofounder and president of Subway, a $2.7-billion sandwich-shop chain, based in Milford, Conn. When he was starting out in 1965 with his first sandwich shop, he paid his meat, bread, vegetable, and paper suppliers in person. All those **face-to-face visits solidified a good relationship with the suppliers**, and when money was tight for the start-up, he told them about it.

As his company grew, says DeLuca, suppliers essentially financed the business, extending credit from a week to up to four months. "They sort of adopted us," says DeLuca. "I suspect that if we were more sophisticated, with once-a-month pay in an envelope with a stamp, we wouldn't have gotten credit."

FINANCE

Quick Pay, Quick Friends

Want better service from your suppliers? Jim Ansara did back when he started Shawmut Design & Construction, in Boston, in the early 1980s. His goal was to differentiate himself from bigger competitors that were pursuing the same subcontractors and vendors. So he figured that **the best way to stand out would be to pay his bills earlier than his competitors**.

Instead of paying suppliers when he got paid by the customer, as most contractors do, Ansara promised to pay within 30 days. Shawmut sometimes had to take out bank loans to make good on its commitment, but as far as Ansara is concerned, the benefits of doing business this way far outweighed the costs.

"It helps position us in the minds of the people we work with. Besides being fair to suppliers, it's been a very good business decision," he says. The policy had an added benefit, too: subcontractors gave Shawmut more attractive pricing because they knew they'll be paid quickly.

Ansara's advice is echoed by Brian Shniderson, of Premiere Merchandising, in Inglewood, Calif. "We never put carrying the business on our suppliers," he says of the bootstrapping days at his promotional goods and services business. "We put it on our clients. We'd tell them we're working our butts off, and we need to be paid within 10 days. We made sure the suppliers got paid no matter what. That way, there's nothing they wouldn't do for us."

224 IDEA

FINANCE

Shipper Anchors Overseas Subcontractors

If you're looking for an offshore manufacturer to subcontract your work to, the people in the middle of your trade—the shippers—may be the best source of leads.

When Joanne Marlowe started a company to sell weighted beach towels, she did business at first with mills in Brazil and Yugoslavia through U.S. agents. But what she really wanted was to **save broker fees by finding offshore mills she could work with directly**. She told her shipper what she was looking for. The shipper then gave her names of contacts at three manufacturers and made introductory calls on her behalf. Marlowe followed up and eventually made the new mills her primary partners.

"When you're dealing overseas, companies are less likely to rip you off if they know you're part of the network," says Marlowe. Bottom line: between cheaper freight and elimination of agent commissions, Marlowe figures she saved 15% to 17% on costs.

VII

"Technology is to the 1990s what mechanical invention was to the Industrial Revolution. The question is not whether you'll use it, but how. And all the ploys to avoid it are just so much wasted energy. You can't experience technology vicariously. You learn about it by immersion."

JOLINE GODFREY
founding partner of An Income of Her Own,
in San Jose, Calif., and author of
Our Wildest Dreams (HarperCollins, 1992)

225
IDEA

COMPUTERS

Battling Computer Viruses

A computer virus is any program that reproduces itself by using the resources of **your** computer without your knowledge. Myths about viruses abound: many people, for instance, think they're contracted primarily through a modem, while software is being downloaded. In reality, as a study by the National Computer Security Association and Dataquest found, floppy disks are by far the most frequent carriers: 65% of viruses that were tracked came through floppies, 25% through local-area networks, 7% by modem, and 1% from preloaded software shipped on the computer.

How do you protect your system? The author of *Robert Slade's Guide to Computer Viruses* (Springer-Verlag, 1994) says: "First of all, back up regularly. Second, **everybody should have antiviral software**; there's no excuse not to get it." Also check every disk and new program you receive, including data files. "Some antiviral software can monitor your system automatically, either all the time or at regular intervals," says Slade. And don't forget to keep your antiviral software up-to-date.

If you detect a virus, there's a good chance you can remove it by running the antiviral scanning program, which should have a "disinfecting" feature. Get rid of the infected file and reinstall it from your backup. And be sure to scan all your diskettes for the virus, or you may reinfect your computer.

COMPUTERS

Overcoming High-Tech Phobia

Getting employees adjusted to their first computers—or even to faster, more complicated computer upgrades—takes a little hand-holding. People hate to feel stupid, and they despise being intimidated by a blinking box.

One way to help workers past the initial frustration is to load their computers with games. **Computer games have helped familiarize people** at Kanon Bloch Carre & Co., an investment-advisory company, in Boston, with using a mouse and learning basic commands. "People get to know how a cursor moves and how to press those keys quickly," partner Richard Fried says, adding, somewhat rhapsodically, that "a bond is created between the uninitiated and the computer." And he says that the games haven't interfered with the real work after they've served their purpose.

227
IDEA

COMPUTERS

Pain-Free Computing

Statistics show that injuries to the wrists, necks, and backs of office-computer users have been doubling every two years since the mid-1980s. There are simple ways, however, to **make a work space more ergonomic** by correcting the positioning of keyboards and telephones, desk measurements, and lighting. A whole industry of books and services has sprung up to offer solutions for making a work space safer and more comfortable for computer users.

Eyes deserve special attention. The American Optometric Association estimates that more than 50% of computer users suffer from sight problems caused by prolonged staring at monitor screens. Computer users should do simple exercises designed to relax and strengthen eyes. For example, doctors recommend that every few minutes, computer users focus on a distant object. If you face a wall, use a mirror.

IDEA 228

MIS Mistakes

I f you've got a growing company that depends on computerization to any degree, **don't put off bringing technical expertise in-house for too long**.

That was the painful lesson learned by Sports Endeavors, a Hillsborough, N.C., direct marketer of soccer and lacrosse supplies. With $26 million in sales, the company was highly dependent on its mail-order software to track orders, customers, and inventory. For years, chief operating officer, Brendan Moylan, relied heavily on his software vendor's expertise and technical support. But by 1994 he was unhappy with the service and decided to make a software conversion. (His timing was excellent: the vendor announced just weeks after Moylan's decision that it was leaving the software business.)

The switch, though, was hell. Moylan scheduled it for the slow season, but it dragged on into the company's busiest time ever, during the 1994 World Cup. When the new system went live, it directed order pickers to the wrong parts of the warehouse. The company fell about two weeks behind in order fulfillment, and with stressed-out employees and angry customers, it lost some $3 million in business.

Everything would have been easier, Moylan suggests, if he'd had a management information systems (MIS) director. Now he does, along with an MIS department. Moylan vows to develop even more in-house expertise.

229 IDEA

COMPUTERS

Lock Up with Backup

Good office security used to mean having a cast-iron safe and a buzzer on the office door. In the electronic workplace, however, the most valuable asset often is information, and safeguarding it requires more than a lock and key.

When most people think of electronic security, they think about hackers—computer jocks who break into other people's files for fun or profit—and viruses, those commands maliciously or mischievously hidden in software that are capable of wiping your hard drive clean.

But hackers account for less than 1% of data losses, estimates Robert Courtney, a computer-security consultant, in Port Ewen, N.Y. Damage from viruses is also relatively trivial, he says. By far, most security-related losses result from blunders—figures entered in the wrong spaces, or files consigned to oblivion or sent to the wrong person by accident. "The crooks are never going to be able to compete with the dummies," says Courtney.

Backing up information will prevent most problems. "You'd be amazed at the number of people running their businesses off personal computers who have no backups," says computer-security expert Lance Hoffman of Washington University, in St. Louis. A number of programs on the market will back up data automatically; there's no excuse not to have one.

REAL
WORLD

"The axiom of 'Never own
anything you can't fix' is
a classic example of what was true
in the industrial era but not in the
information age.
The difference between a buggy
computer program and a faulty
steam engine is that the engine
likely will not work.
By contrast, the program will exhibit
some sort of behavior, and that
behavior will allow you
to debug it."

NICHOLAS NEGROPONTE
professor of media technology,
Massachusetts Institute of Technology
and author of *Being Digital* (Knopf, 1995)

230
IDEA

COMPUTERS

Tap Workers for Computer Capital

I f you're bootstrapping a start-up, you may be able to **get employees to help pay for computers** if they can buy the ones they want. Have them buy the machines and lease them to the company. The company ends up having to invest less capital, and employees get to buy computers partly on the company's tab.

When PTI Environmental Services, in Bellevue, Wash., was starting out, it needed 15 office computers, but CEO Marc Lorenzen could barely afford half that many. So he told his employees that if at least eight of them would buy their own desktop machines, the company would lease them for a year at 50% of the purchase price, which it would pay out monthly. The only restriction was that employees couldn't get anything *too* fancy.

The tactic worked and helped ease PTI over its initial hump. In year two, cash flow allowed the company to buy its own computers, but a few employees refused to switch and volunteered to stay with their own computers at no further charge. Of course, it helped that they had been made stockholders early on, which made clearer the wisdom of pitching in.

COMPUTERS

Overseas Packing

Don't forget when you're traveling overseas and taking along computers, modems, and printers, to **pack adapter plugs and converters**. Adapters allow plugs to fit into differently shaped wall sockets, while converters allow appliances to work with foreign electrical voltages. Often you'll need both, depending on where you're traveling. If you plan to plug a computer modem into a foreign telephone plug, you may also need an additional telephone adapter before you can log on from overseas.

Check with the manufacturers of your equipment for their advice. The travel catalog *Magellan's* (800-962-4943) sells converters and adapter plugs and can make recommendations about what you'll need depending on what countries you'll be visiting.

"My PC is my pen and
paper. My voice mail
is my secretary.
My electronic bulletin
board is my coffee break,
and my fax is my car."

A RESPONDENT
to a 1995 *Inc. Technology* FaxPoll

232 IDEA

The Rapid-Refund Expense Report

People often procrastinate before filling out expense reports—and then want their refund checks immediately, as their credit-card balances edge toward their limits. Particularly for employees away from corporate headquarters, reimbursement can be a real waiting game as the package wends its way through the mail and then through supervisors and an accounting department.

Collectech Systems, a $5-million collection agency, based in Calabasas, Calif., with seven branch offices, figured out a way to expedite the 40 or so expense reports it processes each month. It uses **an electronic expense report**, which essentially is just an adapted spreadsheet. The form automatically adds up the columns and rows and can be E-mailed to supervisors.

The idea came from Collectech's Midwest regional manager, Chris Murphy, who tinkered with a spreadsheet and designed his own expense form. Now standard operating procedure, "the reports are legible, so they reduce error and take less time to check," says Jill Kramer, the accountant who cuts the checks. If a supervisor who needs to approve the report is on the road, the report can be E-mailed out and turned around in hours. The company still needs to keep receipts on file for tax purposes, so accounting holds the check until all the paperwork arrives at headquarters.

233 IDEA

COST CONTROL

Refunds for Going Global

If you're exporting a product that's made with some imported components, ask your customs broker about the U.S. Customs Service's **duty-drawback program**. Under duty drawback, an exporter can get a refund for 99% of the duty paid on the imported item, even if someone else did the importing.

For example, Carstab Products, in Reading, Ohio, was importing an acid from Germany to use in making plastic products. Carstab then exported about 20% of its finished products all over the world and was able to get back nearly 20% of the duties paid on the acid. The refund amounted to about $50,000 one year.

"Duty drawback has been around since 1789," says Harold Lemmesh, one-time chief of the liquidation branch of the San Francisco Customs District. "But there are still probably thousands of companies that have never heard of it."

COST CONTROL

Audit Your Utility Bill

Companies often overlook the excessive expenses that corporate utility bills can create. Surveys suggest that in as many as four out of five cases those bills may include overcharges or other errors.

Thomas Bray, president of PROaudit, a utility-bill audit firm, in Lincoln, Mass., points out that several rate structures are usually available to corporate users. **Don't rely on the utility company to assign you the most cost-effective rate.** "For fast-growing companies especially, it pays to compare various options once a year," says Bray.

When you get your next electric bill, double-check the meter number, meter reading, and meter "constant" (a cost multiplier, recorded on your meter, that helps establish monthly usage). In addition, check to see if you're being penalized for using inefficient machinery that requires a surge of power at start-up. "Because of obscure utility regulations," explains Bray, "you could be billed for more than you use"—charged for kilovolt amps (KVA) needed to fire up equipment, rather than for kilowatts (KW) actually consumed.

235
IDEA

HOME OFFICE

Adapting the Home Phone

Young companies trying to save money often keep their phone bills in check by using one phone line. That's especially the case when entrepreneurs are running businesses out of their homes, using personal phone lines for business as well.

One way to make a single phone line more manageable is to combine it with a service called **"distinctive ringing."** Distinctive ringing gives each of several incoming numbers its own individual ring pattern. The service was originally designed for households with phone-addicted teens, but has been adapted for small offices. You may need to install a special switch to your phone to make the option work; they cost less than $60. Check with your local phone company.

Insuring Home-Based Hardware

A Boston businesswoman realized too late that neither her home-owner's policy nor her automobile coverage would offer much help when her $2,000 laptop was stolen from her car. She was awarded a settlement of only $250. She also found out that her homeowner's policy covers only $2,500 of home business property, which is typical. Until recently, adequate protection for a home office generally meant the purchase of a more costly commercial policy.

See if **your insurance company offers additional coverage for your home office equipment**. One benchmark: Utica National Insurance Group, in Utica, N.Y., (800-274-1914), in conjunction with the Boston Computer Society, offers a rider to its homeowner's or renter's insurance that covers business computer equipment in the home for up to $25,000, at a premium of $5 per $1,000. The policy is all-risk, replacement-cost, and includes a payment of up to $1,000 for expenses incurred in re-creating lost data. The policy will also pay $2,500 for equipment stolen off-premises, which would have helped the aggrieved businesswoman, who had to shell out her own money to replace her laptop.

237
IDEA

HOME OFFICE

Benchmarks for Home Work

Telecommuting is becoming a way of life. **By 1999, more than 80% of all organizations will have at least 50% of their staff telecommuting** in some form—that's according to a 1994 report by the Gartner Group, a Stamford, Conn., consulting firm. Among the report's findings:

- In 1993, there were approximately 7.1 million telecommuters.
- Average work-time increase per telecommuter per day is two hours.
- Typical telecommuting equipment provided by employer includes a 486 PC, fax-modem, telephone line, dot-matrix printer, office furniture, and telephone.
- Average cost for setup is $2,000 to $4,000.

The Flextime Request Form

The number-one issue for employees trying to balance work and personal life is flextime—alternative work arrangements that allow them more control over their schedules and even the option to work at home. The task for employers—from both morale and legal standpoints—is to make sure flextime opportunities are administered fairly.

Work/Family Directions, a $44-million provider of referral services for work-and-family-issues, not only helps its clients grapple with flextime but has had to figure out how to make it work for its own 300-plus workforce as well. One tool that the Boston company has found effective is a form called the **flexible work option request**. The two-page form does not ask why an employee wants flexible work hours—instead, it focuses on the business reasons why the arrangement will or won't work. "You want to get your staff to think about flexibility, not just as a way to accommodate people, but as a way to get good business results," says principal Charles Rodgers.

Among the questions on the form are "How will your proposed schedule sustain or enhance your ability to get the job done?" and "Describe any additional equipment/expense that your arrangement might require. Detail any short- or long-term cost savings that might result from your new schedule to offset these expenses."

"If applicants identify challenges, we want them to think through how they're going to address them," says Rodgers. "The point is to place responsibility for initiating the solution process with the employee."

239
IDEA

HOME OFFICE

Home-Base Basics

"Our fears about at-home workers were that they'd be sipping martinis instead of working," recalls Gary Gagliardi, CEO of FourGen Software, an Edmonds, Wash., company with sales of $8 million. But circumstances forced Gagliardi to give telecommuting a try when the company outgrew its offices and couldn't afford to add space. When three programmers started working at home, Gagliardi required them to keep time sheets, and he carefully monitored their output. But when productivity increased by 25%, he sent seven more workers home to telecommute. The key, he says, is communication: **"We're on E-mail all day**. And everyone attends our weekly meetings."

One consideration for Gagliardi was whether at-home workers are contractors (paid by the job, setting their own hours, and paid no benefits) or genuine telecommuters (full-timers on the regular payroll, whose taxes are withheld and who are eligible for benefits). Telecommuters can be salaried or hourly and eligible for overtime, but either way they should keep records of their hours. Also, some companies may have trouble getting workers' compensation insurance for their at-home workers, because some insurers consider the arrangement an opportunity for fraud.

240 IDEA

High-Class Cost Consciousness

When was the last time you **checked how your business is classified for insurance risk**? As Craig Hickerson discovered, an unchecked mistake can be costly.

Hickerson's lesson came in the form of a bill for workers' compensation coverage at a new branch of his company, Hickerson CATV, a cable-installation business, based in Kansas City, Mo. Instead of the $1.80 per $100 rate he was used to paying, the price had jumped to more than $3 per $100. The reason? The company had been mistakenly classified as a business that strings cable lines between telephone wires, work that's more dangerous than what the company was actually doing. "The insurance salesman thought he could slip it by me," Hickerson says. "I gave him the code we're normally classified under, and he was pretty surprised."

There are hundreds of workers' compensation classifications, with low-end rates for certain clerical workers and high-end rates for bridge workers. There are even hundreds more general-liability classifications. Check with your insurer to be sure your business is properly classified.

241
IDEA

INSURANCE

Detour Insurer Roadblocks

When Mark Moerdler, executive vice-president of MDY Advanced Technologies, in Fair Lawn, N.J., learned that $90,000 worth of computers and equipment had been stolen from his $4-million software and systems-integration company, he figured all he had to do was conduct an audit on the extent of the theft and file the claim with his insurers. Not so. Put off for nearly a year and repaid much less than he had expected, Moerdler offers this advice to small-business managers:

- When you negotiate coverage, **get a full description in writing of whatever documentation the insurer will require** should you have any claims.
- Comparison-shop based, in part, on claims-filing procedures.
- Don't act alone. "Bring in a lawyer at the first sign of delay," advises Moerdler. "I wasted months by not involving our lawyer until the insurer offered us a 50¢-on-the-dollar settlement."
- Take serious measures if your insurer is uncooperative. What finally goaded MDY's insurer into action, says Moerdler, was a threat to report the incident to the New Jersey insurance commissioner, which would have gone into the company's permanent record.

242
IDEA

Two Partners, One Life-Insurance Policy

Mark T. Donohue and Keith D. Greenfield, both in their early 30s, jointly own and operate Symphony Capital Management, a financial-planning business, in Chestnut Hill, Mass. Since they urge their clients to set up buy-sell agreements to ensure orderly transitions when an owner in a partnership dies, it seemed only natural to institute such a plan for themselves. But the cost of purchasing individual life-insurance policies to fund their buy-sell agreement seemed prohibitive—$7,500 per year for the two, says Donohue.

Their solution was to buy an increasingly popular type of **coverage known by the cheery name "first to die."** In Donohue and Greenfield's case, the coverage costs only $2,612 per year for a $500,000 death benefit. "A company buys one of these policies, which covers the lives of all owners, but the policy pays only once, when the first person dies," explains Kenneth Brier, a lawyer with Powers & Hall, in Boston.

Here's the logic: The insurance payoff comes when extra funds are most needed, usually to buy the deceased partner's stock. The payment goes to the surviving partner or the company. It's an excellent option if the surviving partner plans to leave the company to a spouse or sell the business and won't be needing additional insurance funds for future buy-sell agreements.

243
IDEA

INSURANCE

Charming the Cobra

The federal law known as COBRA (Consolidated Omnibus Budget Reconciliation Act) contains a hidden bonus for small companies. There's a provision that allows many of them to save money on the benefits they offer employees hired away from larger companies: they can ask employees to continue their health-insurance coverage with their old company for a year and a half.

Employers are required to offer departing employees that option. The employee has to pay for the coverage, but the tab can't be more than 2% over the employer's cost. Since large companies often have significant rate advantages over smaller companies—as much as 20%—a small company may find that it makes sense to **reimburse new employees for continued health coverage under their previous plans**.

The reimbursements would be taxable income for the employees, which could eliminate the savings to small employers that cover the tax as well as the insurance cost. But COBRA is particularly helpful for start-ups, says William J. Cammock, president of Cammock & Cammock, a benefits-and-compensensation consulting firm, in Cleveland. Some start-ups may find that the law lets them avoid the hassle of establishing health-insurance plans altogether, at least during the early months of operation.

244
IDEA

Working Through Rehab

Do you write off injured workers—approve the workers' compensation claims, find replacements, and say goodbye-for-now to the injured party? You might not have to. **Employees hurt on the job don't have to be lost to workers' comp**. Thomas Lynch, of Lynch, Ryan & Associates, a benefits consulting firm, in Westborough, Mass., and a wholly owned subsidiary of Travelers Corp., says that companies can bring many people who can't do their main task back to work to help with light jobs around the plant or office. That raises productivity, lowers insurance costs, and can boost morale at the same time.

Lynch recommends that you negotiate temporary job descriptions with the injured employee and his or her doctor. In cases in which light or restricted work is possible, Lynch has seen many people accept the offer.

Companies that routinely institute this policy—and have at least 80 to 100 employees insured under what is known as a loss-sensitive plan—can receive refunds of 40% or more on their annual workers' compensation premiums, Lynch notes. Smaller companies usually don't qualify for refunds, but they may eventually get lower premiums.

Harry Featherstone, CEO of Will-Burt, an industrial manufacturer, in Orville, Ohio, credits an early-return-to-work program with cutting his workers' comp claims from $175,000 to just $3,000 annually.

2 IDEA 45

LEGAL

Alternatives to Drug Testing

Drug testing is routinely criticized as being invasive, expensive, and inaccurate. Moreover, it might not catch other, very real, problems. "The majority of accidents are caused by stress and fatigue, not substance abuse," maintains Tammie Fry, human-resources director at Purgatory Resort, a ski and summer resort, in Durango, Colo. Fry says that although her industry is moving toward it, Purgatory has decided not to do random drug testing, opting instead for **computer-based performance testing**.

Employees in such safety-sensitive jobs as ski-lift operation and child care get trained in a kind of PC-based video game, during which they set their own performance "standard." Each day, some 250 of the company's 700 employees take the test before they clock in. The test takes less than a minute, with employees given eight chances to meet their baseline scores. If they miss, they're either assigned different responsibilities or sent home.

Fry says employees "overwhelmingly support the idea over random drug testing." Computer-based performance testing, she says, is also cheaper: the system Purgatory uses costs about $130 per employee for the first year, $64 for each of the next two years, and $27.50 annually after that.

Steps to Discourage Harassment

To discourage sexual harassment in your company, follow these five prescribed steps:

- Adopt a formal policy. Build one around your company's values and the formal definition of sexual harassment issued by the Equal Employment Opportunity Commission. Talk to employees when you distribute it and promise that grievances will be quickly and thoroughly investigated. Explain the disciplinary measures that will be taken against those who harass and against those who bring false charges.

- Provide employees with meaningful recourse. Find two neutral yet powerful people to whom employees can bring grievances. The person in charge of the company is a natural choice, and for the other, pick an outsider who is a close adviser to the business.

- Take all complaints seriously. Investigate promptly.

- Take action. Keep your policy's pledge of disciplinary action, if appropriate. Above all, don't let the complaining employee feel she or he was treated perfunctorily.

- Consider joining with other companies to hire a consultant who can talk to your staff about the issue. Above all, remember that a visible commitment must underpin your program if employees are to take it seriously.

247 IDEA

LEGAL

Keep Trimming Those Legal Bills

When higher interest rates translate into slower collections and pricier loans, business owners need to look for other ways to protect their cash flow. For many companies it's fruitful to make sure that legal expenses aren't padded.

Lynda Graham Mays, president of Ogilvy Management Services, a consulting firm, in Longwood, Fla., says that companies should insist that each bill specifies the start and end dates for itemized services. "Without that information, it's very difficult to audit and to control the cost of any particular legal project," she says.

Ask the firm to identify every person mentioned on your bill, which will help ensure that you're not being billed for dinners that could have been covered more cheaply in 15-minute phone calls. "Companies that take control of their legal relationship by requiring more of this kind of information force law firms to be more accountable," says Mays.

And try to negotiate a money-back guarantee, meaning "the right to audit any bill for up to six months," adds Mays. She recommends you get a written guarantee that your law firm will return all fees that you can prove were unnecessary or excessive.

Heading Off Court

I t's not as if Atlanta Legal Copies were a hotbed of employee lawsuits. It's not, but considering today's litigious climate, management isn't taking chances. The Atlanta-based provider of facilities-management services is **developing its own alternative dispute resolution (ADR) program**.

ADR programs aim to handle employee conflicts before they escalate into costly court cases. Atlanta Legal Copies has taken a three-pronged approach in its program. First, if someone has a problem with a manager, "he or she is automatically entitled to take that concern to the next level," says Joe Carroll, human-resources vice-president. "We guarantee confidentiality, and employees have the option of going as far up the corporate ladder as company president Mark Hawn." Second, the company provides a hotline for employees who have questions about company policy or want to voice complaints. And when all else fails, both sides commit to taking disputes to formal arbitration, where a neutral third party hears both sides and then issues a binding decision.

All new employees are required to sign a document agreeing to compulsory binding arbitration. Current employees—there are 1,600 in 21 states—aren't compelled to sign, but are asked to do so. "It all depends on how you roll it out," says Carroll. "You have to market it and get employees to buy into it."

249
IDEA

LEGAL

Libation Liability

I f an employee gets drunk at your office and then gets in a car accident, your company could be held accountable. "Wherever a company could have controlled alcohol consumption, the company may be liable," says Janet Albers, a lawyer with Rosemary Macedonio & Associates, in Cleveland. That includes employees' drinking in the company's parking lot and at office parties. Ronald Beitman, a Falmouth, Mass., lawyer, concurs: "More courts have been willing to extend liability to employers than to homeowners or other social hosts" because of a perceived "master-servant" relationship between employer and employee.

Both lawyers advise companies to **set clear policies about drinking on site** and to take immediate action if they discover employees are drinking on company property. The Network of Employers for Traffic Safety offers driving safety programs in partnership with the National Commission Against Drunk Driving (202-452-6004).

Entertaining clients over alcohol also has its dangers. "If a company accepts the benefit on its tax returns, then it accepts the burden of the risk," says West Palm Beach lawyer Jeffrey D. Fisher. The only protection a company has is an outright prohibition on *any* drinking.

Break Time

If an employee works so many hours that he or she ends up in an accident because of fatigue, the courts could look your way.

In 1991, in a case called *Faverty v. McDonald's*, an employee worked overnight and into the next day. At 8:21 a.m., he was too tired to continue, and his supervisor let him go. On the way home, the employee had a car accident and died. A jury determined that McDonald's had been negligent and awarded his family $400,000 in damages.

Federal labor law suggests **standards for reasonable lengths of overtime**, but state law may be more stringent. Consult your state labor department for information.

LEGAL

Boomerang from Bankruptcy

If a customer goes bankrupt, acting fast can be the key to recovering any materials you shipped the company directly before the announcement.

You have the right to **reclaim items from a bankrupt company** most of the time. But you have to give the company or bankruptcy court notice within 10 days of when you delivered the goods. The one restriction: you may lose your right to get back your product if it's being used as collateral for an obligation of your once-valued customer.

If your company is in a different city from the bankrupt company, it pays to find someone who will hand-deliver your letter. "Make sure that the letter identifies the items and gives formal notice that you're reclaiming them," says Boston bankruptcy attorney Daniel C. Cohn.

LEGAL

Protecting Your Client Base

I f you run a professional-service business, you've probably faced the problem of employees leaving and taking their—and your—clients with them. Norman Ochelski, who operates his own CPA firm, in Royal Oak, Mich., has a suggestion: **require new hires to sign a contract stating they will pay for clients they leave with**.

"I can't force a client to stay with my company when one of my CPAs moves on," says Ochelski. "After all, client relationships can get pretty close. But I do get fair payment when it happens." Ochelski typically receives one-and-a-quarter times the account's yearly gross billings when a CPA takes the business out the door. The price is based on what the practice would sell for on the open market.

Ochelski has never been taken to court on the agreement, but he says that a friend of his was, and he won the case. The contracts—kind of professional prenuptial agreements—are "not as common as they should be, given how fair and easy to implement they are," says Ochelski. "This way there are no hard feelings when we part company."

253
IDEA

The Subsidiary Shield

If one part of your business carries greater liability risk than others, it may be possible to **protect the rest of your company by spinning it off as a separate corporation**. For it to hold legal water, though, the new subsidiary must be a truly independent corporation.

That means several things: the subsidiary must function independently in its day-to-day operations; it must have sufficient capital of its own to carry on its business; it must have the authority to act in its own best interests, even if they conflict with those of the parent company; customers and other outsiders must understand that the corporations are separate entities and must know which one they're dealing with; and each corporation must observe all the formalities of federal, state, and local laws, as well as its own by-laws.

Of course, would-be plaintiffs may still sue the parent as well as the subsidiary. But if you follow the rules, the courts generally accept that you've made the subsidiary a bona fide legal entity and a viable shield for other parts of your business.

2**54**
IDEA

Supporting Child Support

I n 1994, under the 1988 Family Support Act, states must permit garnishment (the withholding of pay by employers for an employee's
court-ordered child support) from the time when a parent first begins paying support. Complying with the law entails an enormous amount of
bookkeeping for employers, says Helene Brezinsky, a lawyer with the New
York City firm Rosenman & Colin. The court tells the employer what it
must garnish, and the employer then pays the state's collection unit, which
pays the spouse. If an employer has to juggle claims from several former
spouses in several states, the situation gets even more complicated.

Brezinsky's advice is to **be neither too harsh nor too helpful when dealing with
employees facing garnishment**. She has seen employers supply more information on employees than necessary in an effort to facilitate the process.
Other companies accidently make themselves contestants to the case by
trying to help employees. The West Virginia Supreme Court, for example,
held one employer liable for an employee's unpaid child-support payments
and for punitive damages because the employer had agreed to pay the
worker in cash to help him avoid garnishment. For information, call your
state's child-support collection unit.

2*55*
IDEA

LEGAL

What's Your Leave Policy?

The U.S. Department of Labor's Family and Medical Leave Act (FMLA) went into effect in 1993, but **you still have to create your own leave policy** by filling in the details the law has left to each company's discretion. To avoid inconsistencies, misunderstandings, and nasty telephone calls from the Department of Labor, any company with 50 or more employees should consider the following—before any employee requests a leave:

- Under FMLA, companies may require employees to use accrued paid time off as part of the 12-week entitlement. Decide up front if that's what you're going to do, and make sure employees know it.
- Create a clearinghouse for FMLA paperwork, and make sure all supervisors know the procedure for leave requests.
- As an employer you may require medical certification to support a request for leave because of a serious health condition. One caveat: if you ask one employee for proof of serious illness, you must ask all.
- You must continue health coverage for employees on leave, but you may ask them to cover their share of the premiums. If you do, establish a collection process.

For more information, contact the Department of Labor, Employment Standards Administration, by fax, at 202-219-8740.

256
IDEA

Setting Up an AIDS Policy

The best time to write a company policy for employees with AIDS is before someone comes forward with the news that he or she is HIV-positive. After managers from several companies at an industry roundtable mentioned that they had HIV-positive employees, Michael Lauber figured it was time to consider an AIDS policy for his 100-employee company, even though he didn't perceive it as being at immediate risk. With help from the American Red Cross and the National Leadership Coalition on AIDS, in Washington, D.C., Lauber developed **a chronic-illness policy statement for his company**, Tusco Display, in Gnadenhutten, Ohio.

Besides complying with the federal Rehabilitation Act and state and local ordinances covering disability discrimination, employers with 15 or more workers are required under the Americans with Disabilities Act to provide "reasonable accommodations" for those who are HIV-positive or have AIDS. Lauber, for instance, is prepared to discuss short- and long-term disability leave, and an advance on a life-insurance policy. He also holds on-site educational seminars, which have had unforeseen benefits. "One of our managers had jaundice," says Lauber. "Though it had nothing to do with AIDS, his co-workers were prepared to understand that they couldn't 'catch it' from casual contact. People might have been freaked out if they hadn't been educated."

257
IDEA

OFFICE

Big Business's Yard Sale

When software maker MapInfo, in Troy N.Y., needed office furniture, it saved 25% on 150 workstations by **buying at a secondhand office-furnishings company**. Corporate layoffs have fueled an expanding market in recycled office furnishings; some $800 million of product changes hands annually. Consumers can save as much as 80% off original list price for desks, chairs, tables, and panels. And MapInfo says that its renovated equipment not only was as sturdy as new, but was supported by robust customer service as well. The company it bought from helped design the layout of the furnishings and visited after delivery to touch up the goods.

If you're thinking of shopping for refurbished equipment, send for a free directory of recycled-furniture dealers that are members of a trade group trying to centralize a largely mom-and-pop market. The directory's more than 250 entries, listed by region, describe the size, product lines, and services of each facility. Send a request on letterhead to: National Office Products Association, attention Office Furniture Recyclers' Forum. 301 North Fairfax St., Alexandria, VA 22314.

Smooth Move

Moving your office to a new location? **To avoid problems on moving day**, Dorothy Erwin, president of Facility Options/RSI, a consulting company, in Minneapolis, recommends checking these points long before you start packing:

- Does your new location have any rules governing when you can move? Weekend and evening moves are more expensive.
- Are the doors big enough? Erwin recalls a $10,000 conference table so big the company had to get approval from its building's insurance company to put it on top of the elevator.
- Are there adequate dock sites to load and unload furniture and equipment at both your old and new buildings? Will moving trucks fit into the garages?
- Is your mover flexible? Try to get latitude in your contracts with the movers, in case you have to reschedule if the space isn't ready on time. Normally, you'll be subject to a penalty.

259 IDEA

Employees as Office Designers

I f your office needs painting or if you're installing new modular furniture, consider having employees do their own spaces.

When Woodsmith, a Des Moines publisher of catalogs and magazines for do-it-yourself carpenters, upgraded its offices, CEO Donald Peschke asked each of the 35 staff people to help for a weekend. The idea was not so much to save money as to save time. Peschke estimates it would have taken outside installers a week or more to break down the offices' movable panels and modular furniture and put up new ones. Instead, Woodsmith's amateur installation staff began disassembling the old offices on a Friday night and by Monday morning had the redone walls and furniture bolted in place.

With guidance from a designer on loan from a local Herman Miller dealer, each occupant designed a layout for his or her alloted area, considering position of computers, location of work surfaces, and placement of file cabinets and pinup surfaces. "Our approach was to **get them involved in the design** so they'd understand what *couldn't* be done," says Peschke. "People accept limitations a lot better that way, instead of the boss saying 'This is what you're going to live with, like it or not.'"

Another advantage, adds Peschke, who launched the weekend stint with a communal pizza dinner, "turned out to be the camaraderie it developed."

REAL
WORLD

"The biggest impact of technology
has been to allow us to do
unproductive things at a far more
impressive rate. In my day job at
Pacific Bell, I can write a useless
memo and E-mail it to dozens
of people who are too busy writing
their own memos to do anything
about mine. But in general the new
technology has vastly increased
my job satisfaction.
I can spend hours doing stuff like
upgrading my RAM—which I
consider fun—and it looks like
actual work."

SCOTT ADAMS
creator of the cartoon *Dilbert*,
which chronicles the corporate adventures
of an office computer nerd and his smart-ass dog

260
IDEA

OFFICE

Reengineering the (Small) Corporation

If you think reengineering applies only to the cluttered bureaucracies of big business, take a closer look at how things are being done at your own company. Mary Baechler, for instance, figured that she had cut the costs of making her strollers as much as she could at Racing Strollers, her $7-million company, in Yakima, Wash. But when she brought in a consultant, he told her that if she changed some of the basic operations, the fat would just melt away.

So Baechler began **reconsidering hundreds of little details in how her business is run**. In the production area, for example, boxes were being sealed, opened, and resealed every time a different component went inside because they weren't sturdy enough to stand on their own; now the company is trying tabbed boxes. When the company received a fax, it was processed 15 times (logged into a book, copied for Baechler, and so on). "Only after a lot of work did we reduce the number to four," says Baechler. "And it's typical of what we found throughout the company. A French pastry chef had nothing on us! We were the *cordon bleu* of complicated processes."

The hard part is that "if you were to look at all those steps for a fax, every one originally had a good purpose." But the consultant offered moral support, too. "One of the best points our consultant taught us is that people are working as hard and as fast as they can," says Baechler. "They're giving their best effort. It's the system, all those processes, that holds them back."

261 IDEA

Accepting In-House Bids

Next time you sign a check to an outside janitorial or maintenance service, think about addressing it to your own employees.

When Harry Brown, president of Erie Bolt, in Erie, Pa., eliminated his janitorial staff to reduce payroll, he thought of contracting the work out. His employees, though, had a better idea: **they wanted to bid on the maintenance work themselves**. Several people said they wanted the added income and would be willing to do the work after hours and on weekends. What's more, they undercut the outside contractor's prices.

Soon the president of the union was doing the company's snowplowing, and three employees and one retiree were coming in regularly to clean the shop, maintain the equipment, paint, and do minor repairs.

Brown says that there's no doubt the company is getting better service. "The employees know the place better, and if they don't do a good job, they know the other employees will get on their case."

262
IDEA

OFFICE

Are We Having Fun Yet?

People don't even want to talk about accounting, it's so boring," says Yvonne Angelo, cofounder and vice-president of purchasing of SBT Accounting Systems, a $16-million accounting-software company, in San Rafael, Calif. She figured a little levity would go a long way, particularly in a business like hers.

At SBT, **front-desk personnel get a stash of cash to buy yo-yos, candy, and toys** to have hanging around the office. "If employees are relaxed and having fun," Angelo says, "it comes across to our dealers."

263
IDEA

Packaging Popped Fresh Daily

There are alternatives to using those polystyrene peanuts for packaging. Teresa Harrison, founder and president of SET Laboratoies, in Mulino, Ore., found that **real popcorn was just as good a packing material as the plastic stuff**.

When Harrison first made the switch, she included a note explaining her reasoning and pointing out that, while it is popped fresh daily, the packing material is not intended for human consumption. The only hitch was that SET's packaged goods—its software and manuals—had to be enclosed in envelopes, or they would absorb the popcorn smell. But popcorn turned out to be not only kinder to the environment, but cheaper for Harrison's company, too. After the company invested in an air popper, it spent about 60% less for the real popcorn than it had for the fake peanuts, even without buying popcorn in bulk.

264
IDEA

Open for Inspection

I f your employees don't keep their work areas as orderly as you'd like, take a tip from Max DePree, the former chairman of Herman Miller, a *Fortune* 500 office-furniture maker with sales of $1 billion. Back in the 1950s, when Herman Miller was a midsize company, DePree discovered a way to keep the building neat that worked better than nagging or giving orders: **holding open houses for families**. The Zeeland, Mich., company started the practice to help workers' families become more engaged with the company, but DePree noticed that the occasions had a nice side effect. Offices and work spaces got a thorough straightening, as employees prepared for their family guests.

Paper Chase

I n many fast-growing companies, paperwork and the people who handle it are often neglected. Not so, though, at NCO Financial Systems, an $8-million collection agency, in Blue Bell, Pa. There, president Michael Barrist initiated **a bonus system for data-entry clerks** that has brought the paperwork problem under control.

For every day finished without a backlog, each of NCO's dozen clerks gets a point. At the end of the month, prizes of $250, $200, and $150 are awarded to the top three performers. To keep the rest of the staff's spirits up, there's also a random drawing for a $100 prize. "This is a business where usually everybody works to win some prize or contest except the clerks," Barrist says. "This way nobody feels left out of the fun."

With the system in place, productivity increased an average of 25%, which saved on the cost of bringing on an additional clerk. And it was done, says Barrist, with no drop in quality.

266
IDEA

OFFICE

Voice Mail from Overseas

Linking up with your U.S. office when you're overseas can present some technical challenges, but a simple gadget can fix one common problem.

"I do a lot of my business with faxes and phones," says David Blohm, CEO of MathSoft, a software company, in Cambridge, Mass. "But one of the tough things I've found is that lots of European phones don't have touch tones to trigger our voice-mail system when I call in for messages."

Blohm's indispensable take-along is **a pocket tone dialer**. The one he uses is from Radio Shack. Smaller than an audiocassette, it costs about $20. The gadget mimics touch tones: a user holds it to the phone's mouthpiece and punches numbers on the device as if punching numbers on the phone's keypad itself. The tones trigger responses at the voice-mail end, so that Blohm can collect and leave messages as usual.

IDEA

A Third Eye

O ne way to improve productivity is to examine a process and streamline it. That's what Dave Miller, president of Lemco Miller, tried at his $2-million machine-parts manufacturer, in Danvers, Mass. The problem, he says, is that "you forget so much and don't see all the wasted motions." His solution: **use a video camera to capture the process**.

Miller videotaped several tool-setup processes at one milling work center. Watching the tape, he noticed details he'd missed earlier, like workers having to walk back and forth during the setup to borrow tools from other work centers. Getting tools ready beforehand was just the kind of "soft," no-cost procedure change Miller was seeking.

He invited work teams and management to view the tape. As they watched it, people suggested changes like shifting a cabinet that blocked access to equipment and getting all the necessary materials closer to the machines. The tips cut setup time by 15% to 20% throughout the work center, which has meant hours of savings per week.

268
IDEA

Paying for Savings

A big problem with most employee-suggestion systems is that the financial rewards, if they exist at all, tend to be unrelated to the value of the suggestions. Without much incentive to find better ways to do things, people lose interest in trying.

Not so at Peavey Electronics. The Meridian, Miss., company **pays a percentage of projected savings to the person who makes the suggestion**. Peavey, which makes amplifiers and guitars, used to have a more conventional system, rewarding suggestions with $25 to $100 bonuses. But president Melia Peavey says the system was changed to generate more excitement.

At Peavey, hourly workers are paid 8% of the estimated first-year labor and materials savings that result from their ideas. Each month the company's human-resources staff estimates the first-year savings of the 12 best suggestions and then awards the originators of the ideas their percentages up front—"we give people the benefit of the doubt," says Peavey. At a minimum, an employee receives $15. There is no maximum, however. One machinist, for instance, figured out how to reduce the amount of maple scrap created by the neck-carving machine. The company estimated that his suggestion would save the business more than $16,000 the next year, and he received $1,331.

QUALITY IMPROVEMENTS

Check Out the Inside Story

You can't solve problems until you identify their sources. If, for instance, you run a retail chain and sense that a particular store is underperforming, you're likely to get some explanation from the store's manager. But chances are, you'll hear only part of the story. To find out the other part, Richard Schulze suggests you **talk to the checkout personnel by taking them out to breakfast**.

Schulze, CEO and chairman of Best Buy Company, a Minneapolis-based chain of 205 consumer-electronics superstores, has a simple theory: "If you've got a problem, go to the last point the customer visits."

Cashiers hear customer complaints and observe how a store runs, but usually nobody asks their opinions. Schulze says breakfasts are better forums than traditional meetings, because the relaxed atmosphere fosters conversation. And the cashiers consider it a nice treat. For the price of a light meal, says Schulze, he gets "absolutely invaluable results."

REAL
WORLD

"When it comes to management, Peter Drucker is the guy. He's the best. I've read four of his books, and some of the best advice is in *The Effective Executive*. One of the main things that's influenced me is his notion of doing one thing at a time. He pokes fun at people who are executive Mozarts, who think they can do everything at the same time."

WHIT STILLMAN
former ad salesman and current writer, director,
and producer of movies,
including *Barcelona* and *Metropolitan*

IDEA

Paying for Perfection

Sometimes you have to create special incentives to get people to raise their performance a notch. At Jadtec Computer Group, a 36-employee computer-repair business, in Orange, Calif., technicians were fixing computers on the first visit only 80% of the time. That had its costs: customers who weren't happy had to call for another repair, and technicians had to make second visits. So CEO John Dieball set up an **incentive program that rewards people for getting it right the first time**.

Dieball puts 3% of the company's monthly profits into a pool and designed a point system. If technicians fix the computer on the first visit, they get two points. If it takes two or more visits, they get one point. If the case reopens within 10 days, they lose five points. At the end of each month, the profit pool and total points are calculated, and the former is divided by the latter to get the dollar value of each point. The program did the trick: quality at the $6-million company is up, with technicians now tallying a 95% first-time success rate.

QUALITY IMPROVEMENTS

Time Out from New Accounts

When quality is what it takes to get and keep your customers, you need a system to maintain it—which may mean sacrificing growth for a time. Hospital Correspondence Copiers, a $44-million San Jose, Calif., provider of medical record-copying services to hospitals nationwide, **stops taking on new customers if quality dips**.

"Our service is offered on a month-to-month basis," says CEO Scott Hallman, "so customers aren't locked into anything. We have to be vigilantes about quality." The key part of the company's sales pitch is that it won't copy records incorrectly and it won't have late delivery, so if monthly customer checks indicate that quality is dropping, the company has its salespeople stop signing up new customers for six to eight weeks.

The reprieve gives the business the opportunity to hire and train new staff without the pressure of taking care of new clients. And the marketing staff has time to update market analyses, develop new campaigns, and call on prospects without having to close sales. Does the company lose customers? Hallman says maybe 10% of those he turns away during those weeks do look elsewhere. But he thinks that compared with his chief competitor, he does better at keeping the accounts he has.

ISO Gets the GO

The first time Lori Sweningson heard the phrase "ISO 9000" was in 1991, at an annual conference her Minneapolis company, Job Boss Software, holds for its software customers. "One of them asked, 'What are you going to do about meeting ISO 9000, those European quality requirements?' And I thought, 'Beats me.'" Job Boss makes software for small custom manufacturers to manage their shop flow, and "the word was that **to trade in the European economic community**, manufacturers would need to prove that their processes meet minimum quality standards."

Never mind that at the time, Job Boss didn't have any European customers. Some of its customers had European customers, and that was enough to persuade Sweningson to pursue ISO certification, which is like a Good Housekeeping Seal of Approval. (When anglicized, ISO stands for International Standards Organization.)

It took more than a year for Job Boss to complete all the steps of showing how it guarantees quality work. The effort cost upwards of $30,000. But Sweningson says the little changes—along with the big changes—have been worth it: "When you have a blueprint of where you're going, it's so much easier to rally the troops."

273 IDEA

QUALITY IMPROVEMENTS

No-Surprise Quality Control

Even in small companies it's a struggle to keep people informed. But if you've already invested in electronic mail, you might as well use it to its fullest. The 30 employees at Fargo Electronics, in Eden Prairie, Minn., wanted to have daily meetings to keep everyone up on news and to give feedback on quality control. That idea was dropped for a better one: **a daily electronic newsletter**, which president Robert Cummins was sure would be faster *and* more informative.

At the end of each day at the $6-million manufacturer of color and ID cards, department heads jot down messages electronically. The next morning, the messages are compiled into one missive that is printed out and put in the break room. Regular topics include daily sales and production figures, profit-sharing updates, and customer feedback. "It's been great for eliminating surprises," says Cummins. "If problems with a product keep coming up in the newsletter, no one's shocked when we discontinue it."

RETAIL

Open to the Public

You don't have to be a retailer to build a marketing program around location. Steve Ettridge decided to locate his temporary-help offices in storefronts, and he believes the decision was key in making Temps & Co. the largest temp firm in Washington, D.C. "If image is important to your business," he says, "**it pays to have a storefront**."

A few years ago, 4 of the company's 12 locations were in retail space, which costs 20% to 50% more than office space. The company invested in design and decoration of the reception areas that passersby see, which Ettridge insists was well worth the extra cost. "Presenting a professional, upbeat face to the public does wonders for the way people perceive your business."

The storefronts also helped the company meet its biggest challenge: recruiting skilled employees to send out on jobs. Ettridge figures that the company's visibility increases the walk-in rate by 50%.

275
IDEA

Courting the Power Retailers

Mass merchandisers book about 40% of all U.S. retail sales, and discount retailers—chains with 50 stores or more—book 11% to 13% of all retail sales, even though they account for less than 3% of all retail establishments. How do you get your product into their stores? **The road into the power retailers is paved with common sense**:

- To start, ask around to identify absolutely the right contact at corporate headquarters. Marty Burks, a buyer for Sears, is blunt: "If they don't know whom to get the information to, they're not going to get any consideration from me."

- When you call, leave your name. And expect to have to call again, and again. "You'll make six phone calls before you get a call back," warns Best Buy merchandising manager Bob Griffin.

- Go to trade shows, where the buyers you've been playing phone tag with will be. "I like to see people we'd otherwise never be exposed to," says Target buyer Teri Kohler. When you make your pitch, says Best Buy's Griffin, the most important point to get across is that you know your customer and your competition. "If you're not customer driven, nothing else matters."

- When you promise to send something, send it, pronto. And then make sure you're ready, with promotional ideas and an advertising allowance, if one of the major retailers calls back.

276
IDEA

Speedy Checkout

Sometimes a customer's final impression is the one that really counts. That's why Elliot Goodwin, president of Larry's Shoes, a 10-store chain of shoe stores, based in Fort Worth, Tex., **took steps to reduce customers' time at the cash register**. Larry's spends $500 a month to keep an open phone line between its mainframe computer and a credit-card clearinghouse so that there is never a busy signal. When a customer pays with plastic, credit confirmation takes only five seconds instead of perhaps a minute—a minuscule benefit by some measures, but part of Goodwin's determination to impress the customer.

Meanwhile, using CD-ROMs containing white-page telephone listings for local markets, MIS director Tom Thomason loaded the mainframe computer with 450,000 names, addresses, and phone numbers of non-customers within the areas where Larry's operates. Those names were combined in a database with the 650,000 customer names the company already had. That way, when a customer goes to check out, the cashier only has to key in the phone number, and the computer automatically pulls up a name and address.

Goodwin says it's hard to measure the return on the upgrades to the $31-million company. "Some of it is blind faith that the money I'm investing will pay off," he says. "We're trying to look at things through the customer's eyes, to enhance the experience in the store. If we don't have good customer service, everything else is just window dressing."

TECH
TIP

277
IDEA

RETAIL

The Daily Due Date

A maternity-clothing company has figured out a clever way to afford good retail real estate: it **rents small spaces, stocks limited inventory, and is committed to replacing that inventory daily**.

Mothers Work is a Philadelphia-based retailer of upscale maternity clothing. Rebecca Matthias, founder and president, experimented at first with a mail-order catalog. Although that approach didn't work, it got her to think about retailing in a nontraditional way. She realized that a free-standing maternity store had to be small to justify its low traffic, but it needed a wide selection because mothers-to-be make several purchases at once. So the 84 Mothers Work stores stock only one of each size of all but the best-selling items, which saves space. Then, using software designed for mail-order businesses, the company tracks daily store sales by item and sends replacement inventory by UPS.

Matthias developed her just-in-time inventory system to adapt to the economics of her industry, but it has an added benefit: quick response to customers. Mothers Work manufactures more than 75% of the items it sells, but it's never caught with huge amounts of excess inventory. Using a network of Philadelphia stitching contractors, the $60-million public company can swiftly manufacture more of the items and colors that sell well. "It keeps us very close to our customer," says Matthias.

VIII

"Lifestyle is an integral part of business. If you can't grow a business both profitably and in a way that you can look at yourself in the mirror and say, 'Yes, I like the person I am,' and you can look at your whole company and say, 'This is a whole company where the people who work here, who are our internal customers, enjoy being those customers,' then I don't think it's worth doing."

BEN NARASIN
founder and president,
Boston Prepatory Co., in New York City

278
IDEA

Organizing a Contest for a Cause

Every businessperson can think of a way to link his or her company to the community. For Jacki Baker, co-owner of Mother Myrick's Confectionery & Ice Cream Parlor, in Manchester Center, Vt., it was a question of reaching her primary customer: she **wanted to do something to encourage children to read**.

So Baker and her husband, co-owner Ron Mancini, set up a reading game at their ice-cream shop (the company also sells candy by mail order). Local high-school art students designed a game sheet on which grade-school children could write down the names of books they had read. The artist whose design was chosen received a $50 savings bond. Then the company got teachers to distribute the sheets to 2,000 students in the surrounding area. Every time a child read two books, he or she could collect an ice-cream treat from Mother Myrick's. After reading 11 books, children and their families got a free cake and ice cream.

More than 300 children took part. "Parents told us kids were holed up in their rooms reading," says Baker. The project cost less than $3,000 and raised the company's profile. Commendations came from the chamber of commerce, Vermont's then-governor Madeleine Kunin, and literacy advocate Barbara Bush.

279
IDEA

Encouraging Volunteerism

If you want to get your company involved in your community but either can't afford cash donations or want to give something that won't be forgotten as easily, think about **giving employees time off to do volunteer work**. Clay Teramo is one of many company owners who's done it. Even when his company, Computer Media Technology, in Sunnyvale, Calif., was just a $2.7-million business with 13 employees, people were taking paid time off to volunteer The company averaged about one person for one afternoon a week.

For people who didn't have a favorite charity, the company posted a list of local organizations, such as a soup kitchen and a home for the elderly, with a note asking for advance notice if they want to help out. "We don't want to just give our money away," says Teramo "And that would miss out on the intangible rewards anyway. Volunteering helps keep work from becoming a grind." He gives some of his time himself to charitable fund raising, providing sales and marketing help.

280
IDEA

COMMUNITY

Being a Good Neighbor

Bryan Beaulieu, CEO of Skyline Displays, an $81-million manufacturer of portable trade-show exhibits, in Burnsville, Minn., was looking for **a way to unite his employees and independent distributors**. "We had drifted apart," he says. So, for the annual meeting, Beaulieu organized a project everyone would remember: building a playground.

Residents close to the company's headquarters volunteered time and equipment, and employees and distributors donated engineering and carpentry skills over four days. The event was filmed, and the tape is used for recruiting.

Today, Skyline Displays has 350 employees and 1,000 distributors and representatives. "Whenever we have a bad day," says Beaulieu, "we go down to the park, watch the kids playing, and get revitalized."

FAMILY

Relearning to Shift Gears

Although it's hard not to think about business when you come home to your family, you'd better figure out a way to **focus on the people you care about when you're around them**—or they might stop trying to connect with you at all.

"Many years ago, I was sitting at the dinner table with my wife and three children—something I didn't do often," says Bill Deimling, president of Deimling/Jeliho, a plastic-injection-molding company, in Amelia, Ohio. "My oldest daughter was busy telling me about something that had happened in school that day. I didn't hear a word she said. When she finished, I started talking to my wife about my day without so much as a comment about my daughter's. She left the table, and I never even noticed until she was already walking away." Deimling then asked her about school. She replied, "Dad, I already told you, but I knew you didn't hear. Nothing counts but the business."

From that night on, Deimling resolved to change, to "stop being a provider and start being a father." He took up coaching his kids' soccer and softball teams, made school events a priority, and decided, with his wife, to try not to talk about business at home, especially at the dinner table. "The business took care of itself quite nicely without me for those short periods of time when my children needed to know that they were more important than the business," says Deimling.

282
IDEA

FAMILY

Balancing Family and Business

Entrepreneurs show a remarkable capacity for letting their businesses screw up their personal lives—remarkable mainly because steps toward solutions are often so simple.

Norman and Elaine Brodsky's family life took a beating for years when their businesses were first thriving: Norm says he was unable to coordinate his business schedule with his personal commitments and ended up missing events like music recitals and school open houses.

Finally, the Brodskys came up with a plan to solve the problem. At the beginning of each month, Elaine gives Norm a **computer-generated calendar of family and personal appointments** for the next 30 days, which he incorporates into his business calendar. (Their current company is CitiPostal, in Brooklyn, N.Y.; Norm is CEO and Elaine is vice president of customer relations.) "This way, Norman can decide what he wants to be part of and work his schedule around it," says Elaine. "It saves a lot of headaches." Says Norm: "My life is a lot better balanced than it's ever been."

TECH
TIP

Family-Friendly Office

Child care for two-career couples and single parents is one of the most daunting issues that parents and businesses face. Some large companies have on-site day-care centers; more realistic options for smaller companies include help in making day-care referrals, providing child-care reimbursement as part of a flexible benefit plan, and taking out "company spaces" in day-care centers for lease to employees.

Some companies even find it feasible to **have parents actually care for infants at the office**. That's what worked for Bill Brecht, who owns a BMW dealership, in Escondido, Calif. The company didn't need a child-care license in California as long the children were being cared for by their parents. So the company tried it: it spent less than $500 on playpens, infant swings, play gyms, and two doors, and brought on the babies. Brecht calls the experiment "a resounding success. It sent a spark throughout the store, breathing new life into the place."

On-site care can work when the parent is the CEO, too. When Andrea Cunningham, head of Cunningham Communication Inc. (CCI), in Santa Clara, Calif., had her first child in 1991, CCI employed 52 people and had revenues topping $5 million. Cunningham wanted to keep working but she also wanted to see her child. So she hired CCI employee Alex Chisholm to be her "manny" after he proofread her nanny application and asked for the job. Chisholm cared for the baby full-time and spent half his hours at the office, editing the company newsletter and doing industry research with the baby perched on his hip.

284
IDEA

FAMILY

Keeping Kids a Priority

Don't worry about all the time you spend at your business. It's OK. Your family can do without you for a while.

At least that's the rationalization that passes for reality in many entrepreneurial minds. There's only one catch. "It's just not true," warns Thomas Davidow, a family-business psychologist, in Needham, Mass.

Families need undivided attention as much as businesses. One habit worth cultivating: **set aside at least one evening a week for a dinner date** that everyone can look forward to and depend on. According to Davidow, such commitments often work out well. "Give entrepreneurs a place to be and a goal to accomplish, and you're speaking their language."

Some company builders bring their children along on business. Traveling for his consulting business nearly 75% of the time, Max Carey, owner of Corporate Resource Development, in Atlanta, invites each of his three teenage children to join him at least twice a year on a business trip. "It's uninterrupted one-on-one time," he says. "You end up doing or talking about things you never would at home "

Trade Show Savings

While trade shows may be great for business, they can be disruptive for families when spouses get left behind. One solution: **invite spouses along in return for staffing your company's booth** for a few hours, says Jim Ake, founder of Electronic Liquid Fillers, a $15-million manufacturer in LaPorte, Ind.

Ake figures that a typical bill for a couple of temps to hand out promotional materials in the booth comes to about the same amount as airfare and meal expenses for two spouses. Besides, the spouses have a much better grip on the business and can better answer questions from trade-show attendees. So the company asks for volunteers to come along to shows.

"We like to keep the money inside the company family if it's possible," says Ake, whose company employs 119 people. "When you try to make people's lives better, then they try to make the company better."

FAMILY

Three Steps to Borrowing from Family or Friends

Charles Bodenstab likes to keep his revolving credit line at his bank as open as possible. So to meet his short-term cash requirements, Bodenstab, president of Battery & Tire Warehouse, in St. Paul, Minn., taps sources closer to home: his children, friends, and 40 employees. He's borrowed as much as $100,000 this way, offering the "commercial paper" in $10,000 bites.

Borrowing money from family or friends, of course, can be dangerous. To ensure that the agreement stays professional and that people with limited investment experience don't get caught up in something they'll later regret, Bodenstab follows three rules:

- He gives investors letters acknowledging their investments.
- He pays out attractive interest—say, 1% a month on a $10,000 investment—that about equals his incremental borrowing cost. (In setting an interest rate, he considers not only what the cost would have been to borrow the money from other sources, but also the fact that the money keeps him from having to pay late fees to vendors.)
- He includes a clause that allows investors to get their money back at any time. "All they have to do is let me know," says Bodenstab. "We pay them instantly."

287 IDEA

Insider's Guide to Harmony

One of the most difficult parts of running a family business is figuring out how to encourage some family members to join the company and how to tell others that they need more experience. Typical company rule books offer little guidance. To help make things clearer, one family-run business thought through and came to decisions on issues such as executive and director qualifications, pay scales, retirement ages, and employment opportunities. Then the company wrote the information down—along with some entertaining family history—in what it calls the **family consensus statement**.

The document used by Multiplex, a $28-million manufacturer, in Ballwin, Mo., isn't legally binding, but it does address commonly asked questions. At first, a few of the 22 family stockbrokers refused to sign off on it, which meant that there were still tough issues that had to be wrestled with. But the document forced those issues out in the open. Eventually consensus was reached, and everybody accepted the statement.

"To my great surprise, nieces and nephews can cite it," says J.W. Kisling, chairman and CEO. "It was definitely worth the trouble."

288
IDEA

GIVING

Scoping Out Donations

Charity solicitations, especially requests from local organizations, can be troublesome for CEOs of growing companies. You want to be generous, and you may even fear your business's reputation will be harmed if you're not, but you can't afford to give to everybody.

Handle it as you would any challenge: set up a plan. **Decide once a year how much you'll be giving and to whom.** That's what David Mona, chairman of Mona Meyer McGrath & Gavin (MMMG), a Minneapolis public-relations firm, does.

Since the late 1980s, the company has had a policy for giving. It allocates specified portions of pretax earnings to a few selected organizations and makes its largest contributions by taking on three pro bono accounts each year.

Now, when other groups make a pitch to MMMG's managers, they politely say no, citing their policy of committing themselves heavily to their chosen accounts. "It cuts out all the hemming and hawing," says Mona. "We are spending our dollars more wisely and can decline more kindly. We can say, 'Sorry, we've made a decision, and we're fully committed in that area.' Not simply, 'We aren't interested,' or 'We don't care.'"

GIVING

Art for Business's Sake

One way to get a unique benefit out of a charitable contribution is to donate money to an art museum—some have programs that allow companies to **borrow art for their offices in return for donations**.

For example, the Boston real estate investment firm of Aldrich, Eastman & Waitch (AE&W) was lent 20 original prints and paintings in exchange for a $5,000 donation to a local museum. "For a relatively modest contribution," says William Helm, AE&W president, "we get art that would require enormous investment if we were to buy it." Not only that, but when the firm moved to larger quarters, museum experts came in and designed wall space and lighting for free. The company also got some good publicity by hosting after-hours art shows when the work first went up.

Museums that have lent work in the past include the DeCordova Museum and Sculpture Park, in Lincoln, Mass.; the Los Angeles County Museum of Art; the Whitney Museum of American Art, in New York City; and the Orlando Museum of Art. Some lend from collections, and others lend from special galleries of emerging artists. Some even offer lease-to-buy deals, in case you fall in love with a particular work.

290
IDEA

GIVING

Year-End Thanks

For many businesses, the only competitive factor more important than quality and service is price. So it would be uncharacteristic to throw money around in gifts to customers at the end of the year.

Tom Hillman, president of the Fresh Fish Co., in St. Louis, believes that's the case. "I'm ambivalent about this end-of-the-year gift-giving thing to begin with," he says. "We're just not into doing frivolous things that end up looking like you're trying to buy somebody's business. So we tend to be real tight when it comes to gifts." Once Hillman sent some of his customers copies of a $50 book containing limited-edition drawings of fish, but that was just one year out of many.

Instead, "each year we **send a personal letter to each of our customers**, expressing our thanks for their support during the year," says Hillman. The company also makes a donation to a charity and tells its customers that that's where it's putting its money, instead of fancy holiday cards. One year, for instance, the charity was the American Heart Association, "which made a nice tie-in for those of us in the fish business," says Hillman. Response has been positive. "Customers respect it," he says.

291
IDEA

Children Having Children

There's a wave of company builders who are starting businesses when they're barely out of college, even high school. It's hard to quantify the phenomenon; no one keeps track of the numbers. But the ripples are starting to show up in the *Inc.* 500: in 1992, 30 of the 500 fastest-growing companies in the United States were headed by people 30 years old or younger.

Starting a company when you're in your twenties presents special challenges. "People had a hard time taking me seriously," recalls Bud Prentice of Applied Computer Technology, in Fort Collins, Colo. "A supplier once asked me, 'Where are your parents?'" For many, a big hurdle is money. Few young entrepreneurs have personal savings or collateral to borrow against ("What was the bank going to take, our *stereos*?" asks John Chuang of MacTemps, in Cambridge, Mass.), which means being crafty at bootstrapping or persuading family members that the business is a decent investment.

Still, **most young entrepreneurs believe that they're at the best age to launch a business**. Many don't have a spouse or children to worry about when they're logging 80-hour weeks. Sharing apartments with roommates or even living at home with parents keeps overhead low. And if the business fizzles, when else is it as easy to pick up the pieces? "The worst thing that would happen," figured Bob Roscoe of MBS Communications, in Cheshire, Conn., "was that I'd have to go out and get a job like other people."

292

IDEA

• BEYOND BUSINESS •

LIFESTYLE

When Every Employee's an Entrepreneur

The best thing you can do for your employees may have nothing to do with compensation, benefits, or training. Instead, it may be to help them understand the changing economic landscape, and **the changing nature of work itself.**

That's according to William Bridges, author of *JobShift: How to Prosper in a Workplace Without Jobs* (Addison-Wesley, 1994). "The change I am describing—let's call it 'dejobbing'—has already happened" at companies including Intel, Microsoft, Sun Microsystems, and Apple Computer, writes Bridges. Statistically, in-house and benefits-providing jobs are slowly beginning to disappear. Bridges's advice to employers and people who think of themselves as employees sounds radical to many ears: we need "to address head-on the issue of people holding on to their jobs." The work world of the future, he argues, will be populated by people who consider themselves "in business for themselves" and who, essentially, contract themselves out to employers. The wise company "will work with those microbusiness people collaboratively."

Workers, meanwhile, must become prepared to "act like people in business for themselves by maintaining a plan for career-long self-development, by taking primary responsibility for investing in health insurance and retirement funds, and by renegotiating their compensation arrangements with the organization when and if organizational needs change." Companies that really care about their people, argues Bridges, will help them see and prepare for these tidal changes.

REAL WORLD

"I made a pact with caffeine awhile ago. I swore on an espresso pot that I would drink it every day. Remember, caffeine is your friend. Caffeine cares about you. Caffeine loves you. Caffeine wants you to be happy. You can trust caffeine. Caffeine is the only thing standing between me and the evil personality that I really am."

MARY BETH CONNELLY
former *Inc.* staffer

293
IDEA

LIFESTYLE

Making Connections

A deluge of people are creating home-based businesses and "virtual" companies with their colleagues working out of their own homes across the country or even around the world. It can be heady stuff, but it also can be painfully isolating. The key to staying sane is to network.

Vivian Shimoyama, proprietor of Breakthru Unlimited, a jewelry business, in Manhattan Beach, Calif., is so busy making contacts, joining groups, chairing meetings, collecting business cards, and augmenting her already voluminous database of names that she rarely has a moment to worry about it. "I don't have time to feel lonely," says Shimoyama, who boasts an electronic Rolodex of more than 10,000 names.

"I have a **database of every person I've ever met at a conference or meeting**," Shimoyama says. Her process after meeting people is to follow-up, call, get together for a meeting, then let the relationship germinate—or not. "It's got to be reciprocal," she says. "I've got to think, to whom can I introduce them?" The process is exhausting, but Shimoyama believes she wouldn't have a business without it. "If you go solo and you're not willing to do this," she says, "you're not willing to be in business. You can't survive in solitary confinement."

LIFESTYLE

Making Flying Solo Smoother

More and more people are going into business for themselves, either as a sideline to their full-time work or as their main source of income. Either way, experienced soloists—people who start out by themselves and intend to keep it that way—say that this way of working has its own built-in stresses.

"Starting a business alone can be lonely," says Jane King, a financial consultant who runs Fairfield Financial, in Wellesley, Mass. "Anybody coming from a corporate environment the way I did is used to having a shoulder to cry on on a bad day or collecting a pat on the back on a good day. You lose that."

What's necessary, say King and others who have gone through it, is to get out of the house, to connect with other entrepreneurs and advisers, and to build a new way of getting support. "It is very important to find other people who are like you," says King. "**You need a consortium of mentors and trusted confidants**, people who can console you when business is lousy but who can also give you useful advice—tell you yes, it's normal to worry this much about the business, or no, that software program is not a good investment."

295
IDEA

Home Sweet Homebase

Most entrepreneurs start their companies in whatever town they happen to be living. But sometimes the city you're living in can feel all wrong. That was the case with Bob Freese and three colleagues from 3M, in St. Paul, Minn., when they set out to start a company to manufacture optical-storage devices for computers. The cost of doing business in Minnesota was high, and they'd learned at 3M that A-list recruits were reluctant to move to so cold a climate, even for a job with one of the world's premier corporations. How could a start-up attract good people?

Engineers all, Freese and his colleagues did a **methodical search for a home base**, compiling data on cities across the United States, considering high-tech infrastructure, quality of life, transportation, and talent pools. In the end, they settled on Research Triangle Park, in the Raleigh-Durham area of North Carolina, to launch their company, Alphatronix.

The emerging interest in entrepreneurship in the region clinched the deal for Freese. "A small company coming into this area gets a lot of help from an organization like the Council for Entrepreneurial Development, all of it free," Freese says. You go back to the mid-1980s, he notes, and the hot spots were Silicon Valley, Southern California, and Boston. "But Cleveland, Kansas City, Raleigh-Durham—they all have a reasonably good quality of life, good transportation, good educational systems, a favorable climate for start-ups," says Freese. His main point: there's no need to consider your location a *fait accompli*.

LIFESTYLE

Oh, That Aching Back

More and more, executives are missing work days because of back pain. That's according to orthopedic surgeon Stephen Hochschuler, founder of the Austin-based Texas Back Institute (TBI), the country's first for-profit entity devoted exclusively to the human spine. Many people carry stress in their backs. Furthermore, the increase in the number of hours execs are spending in front of computers is putting new strains on not-so-new bodies.

Some of TBI's pointers: provide vertically adjustable chairs, so hips and knees line up while feet stay flat on the floor. When sitting, place a rolled-up towel at the small of the back. Adjust computer screens so they're at eye level. If you use a phone a lot, get a headset: extensive cradling of a handset strains neck muscles. And **avoid sitting too long: no other position puts so much strain on back ligaments and disks**.

"We try to educate people that the back is no different from the heart," says Hochschuler, "in that pain is a sign you're in trouble and you should see someone about your lifestyle." TBI offers a free Back Pain Hot Line (800-247-BACK).

297 IDEA

LIFESTYLE

A Business Plan for Life

Most entrepreneurs are careful about making sure they know where their companies are going and how what they're doing today in the business will have a payoff tomorrow. But how many people can say the same thing about their life? Every businessperson, contends Sheila West, should **write a "business plan" for his or her personal life**.

West, CEO of ACI Consolidated, a Monroe, Mich., distributor of archery equipment and an *Inc.* 500 company, uses a different phrase to describe what she means: she calls the personal business plan a "purpose statement." She outlines a statement for each of the roles she plays: mother, wife, community leader, company CEO, and more. For each role, West has considered and articulated how she hopes to grow and where she wants to be, and she sets tangible goals and lists steps toward attaining them—just as she does when she sets goals for her business. Periodically she rereads what she's written to gauge her progress.

"Vision gives us hope that our needs can be met and inspires us to make our dreams become reality," says West in her book *Beyond Chaos* (NavPress, 1991).

REAL
WORLD

The secret to a
productive sabbatical?
"Make sure you don't get
anything accomplished
while you're away from
your company.
Do absolutely nothing."

BEN COHEN
cofounder of Ben & Jerry's Homemade,
in Burlington, Vt.

298
IDEA

LIFESTYLE

Rewarding Yourself

I f all that risk and hard work you weathered in starting a company has begun to pay off and you want to reward yourself—say, with a snazzy car—should you worry about the message it sends to employees?

"The issue is one of morale, not morals," says Gary Edwards, president of the Ethics Resource Center, in Washington, D.C., which provides consulting to businesses and government. "You have an obligation to pay employees fairly, but as an owner, you took the risks and should reap the rewards."

Chuck Piola, executive vice-president of sales for NCO Financial Systems, in Blue Bell, Pa., agrees. He drives a Mercedes but makes sure everyone knows his story. "Apologize for getting rich," says Piola. "Say, 'Listen, I'm uneasy with something. I've worked hard, and I want to reward myself.'"

On the other hand, Mirit and Josef Rabinovitz, founders of JMR Electronics, in Northridge, Calif., don't believe there's anything to apologize for. They heard grumbling when they bought a Mercedes, but laughed it off. "If you become defensive, that legitimizes their objection," they say.

A Personal Search

Why do people start businesses? Sometimes for money, sometimes to find independence, but often because of something more deeply rooted. Catherine "Kye" Anderson **traces her origins as an entrepreneur** to a personal tragedy and the abiding passion that grew out of it. And she says that realizing that connection has made her work more meaningful.

It took 10 years in business before Anderson ever consciously made the link between the company she founded in 1977, Medical Graphics, a $23-million St. Paul, Minn., maker of heart and lung diagnostic equipment, and her father's death. When Anderson was 13, her father suffered a massive coronary. Just days before he died, doctors had insisted his shortness of breath was unrelated to his heart. "I remember sitting on the radiator by his bed and a doctor coming by to read an EKG machine," says Anderson. "The picture of that doctor trying to make sense of a squiggly line and not knowing what was wrong haunted me for years." Anderson became a medical technologist and then developed software to translate diagnostic measurements into easily read computer graphics.

"Many entrepreneurs are driven by some experience they keep buried deep down," says Anderson, who is chairman, CEO, and president of her publicly owned company. "But it's important to recognize it and share it. It gives you a clarity of vision."

300 IDEA

Pre-Partnership Pondering

You may be reluctant to **discuss the potential breakup of your business partnership**, fearing that such talk could prove self-fulfilling. But clarifying sticky questions while you're all on good terms can help prevent some of the tension that leads to business divorce. And if you *do* decide to split, written agreements can help ensure that everyone's treated fairly.

"There's an assumption by many partners that no matter what happens to their businesses, they'll be partners forever," says lawyer David Gibbs, of the Boston law firm Peabody & Brown. Even when his clients have the best of intentions, Gibbs still advises them to set up an agreement detailing how they'd establish the worth of company stock if one partner wanted out, what each would do if the other died, and how to govern the sale of stock to outsiders. For small companies, most such agreements cost between $1,000 and $4,000, says Gibbs.

There's another benefit to the exercise. People who can't come to terms on how they'd get out of their relationship have a second chance to think about getting into one.

TIME MANAGEMENT

Making the Most of Travel

Jimmy Calano, cofounder and CEO of CareerTrack, an $80-million seminar company, in Boulder, Colo., is like most company managers when it comes to business travel: he thinks that most deal making needn't be done in person. He'll ask the person he's dealing with if an in-person visit is necessary. "I'll say, 'I'm willing to make this trip, but is it the best use of your time? Do you have two or three hours to give me if I come?'"

When he is away from the office, Calano abides by four habits that help him stay efficient. First, he staples a mini-itinerary to his plane-ticket jacket that includes information on his flight numbers and times, hotel, and airport transportation. Second, he maintains his daily business routine, which means getting a fax by 6 a.m. of the previous day's sales. Third, he checks in with his assistant at two—and only two—predesignated times a day.

And fourth, Calano **designs an agenda of what will be covered at his meetings** and in which order, and faxes it ahead of time to his host. "An agenda gives you power," says Calano. "When you have that agenda, it makes you look well prepared, and it conveys that you're very serious. It's a simple way to set yourself apart." It also helps you figure out when the meeting is over· "Once you've covered that last issue, that's it."

A

ABC Supply 27
ABL Electronics 56
Accion International 187
Acclimator Time 42
Accu Bite Dental
Supply 142
ACI Consolidated 63, 338
ADM Technology 48
Advanced Products
& Technologies 17
Alan Gaynor & Co. 22
Aldrich, Eastman
& Waitch 329
Allen Systems 195
Alphatronix 336
American Design
& Manufacturing 213
American Fastsigns 185
American Optometric
Association 262
American Red Cross 293
American Society
of Association
Executives 18
American Society
for Training and
Development 180
American Sweeteners 228
American Teleconferencing
Services 138
An Income of Her Own 259

Andover Advanced
Technologies 216
Applied Computer
Technology 331
Approach Software 78
AquaSource 187
Arcon Manufacturing 46
Artful Framer Gallery 60
Arthur Andersen 101
Artistic Impressions 204
Aspen Institute 187
Atlanta Legal Copies 285

B

Babybag of Maine 69
Baird 64
Barnstable Grocery 40
Battery & Tire
Warehouse 326
Beers & Cutler 222
Ben & Jerry's
Homemade 172, 339
Berthelot & Associates 94
Bertucci's 177, 226
Best Buy 307, 314
Bombay 251
Boston Computer
Society 273
Boston Metal Products 47
Boston Prepatory 317
Bread Loaf
Construction 146
Breakthru Unlimited 334

Brooktrout Technology 151
"Bugs" Burger Bug
Killers 80
Business Wire 84
Buy Networks 125
BXI 191
Byrne Companies 157

C

California Delivery Service 57
Calyx & Corolla 37, 75
Cammock & Cammock 280
Cannondale Europe 44
Carbide Surface 98
CareerTrack 235, 343
Carstab Products 270
CE Software Holdings 26
Checkfree 106
Cherry Tire Service 102, 122
CitiPostal 32, 250, 322
Clos LaChance Wines 53
CME Conference Video 133
Collectech Systems 269
Columbia National Bank 120
Com-Corp Industries 137
Community Bank
of Homestead 139
Comptronix 237
Computer & Communications
Industry Assoc. 100
Computer Media
Technology 319
Copy America 130

Corporate Resource
   Development 324
Cray Research 153
Creative Bath 168
Crescent Metal Products 95
Cunningham
   Communication 323
Currency/Doubleday 25, 134

D

Dallas Cowboys 207
Danbury Plumbing
   Supply 168
Dataflex 143
Dataquest 260
Davis, Hays & Co. 232
Deimling/jeliho 321
Delta Audio-Visual
   Security 72
DeMar Plumbing, Heating
   & Air-conditioning 114
Diesel Technology 233
Digital Equipment 223
Dolin & Modica 140
Domain 68
Drenttel Doyle Partners 24

E

Edson 119
Electronic Controls 113
Electronic Liquid
   Fillers 35, 49, 325
Eli's Chicago's Finest
   Cheesecake 120
Elyria Foundry 249
Engineering Design
   & Sales 169

Epstein Becker & Green 129
Erie Bolt 299
Eriez Magnetics 96, 162
Ernan Roman Direct
   Marketing 36
Ethics Resource Center 340
Everyday Learning 183

F

Facility Options/RSI 295
Fairfield Financial 335
Fantastic Foods 166
Fargo Electronics 312
Federal Express 30, 75
FireFly Flashcards 83
Fishers Office Plus 29
Flash Creative
   Management 152
FourGen Software 276
Franklin International 231
French Rags 240
Fresh Fish 330

G

Gardener's Supply 172
Gartner Group 274
Geerlings & Wade 218
General Magic 175
Geneva Business
   Services 221
Globe Metallurgical 229
G.O.D. 109, 155
Granite Rock 236
Grant Thornton 194
Greenville Tool & Die 243

H

Hale and Dorr 43
Harper Companies 85
Heatway 161
Hemmings Motor News 123
Henderson's 101
Herman Miller 296, 302
Hermanoff & Associates 83
Hickerson CATV 277
HiFi Buys 23
Hornblower Dining
   Yachts 185
Hospital Correspondence
   Copiers 310
HRStrategies 159

I

IDB Communications
   Group 15
Illinois Retail
   Merchants Assoc. 101
Indus Group 135
Industrial Steel 238
Integrated Genetics 127
Intuit 55

J

Jackson & Co. 86
Jadtec 309
Jane Ink 188
JMR Electronics 340
Job Boss Software 311
Joe Boxer 106
Johnsonville Foods 145
Jostens Learning 220
Just Desserts 124
J.W. Pierson 31

K

Kanon Bloch Carre
& Co. 261
Kaplan Educational
Centers 54
Key Medical Supply 41
Kingston Technology 129
Koss Corp. 71
Kronish, Lieb, Weiner
& Hellman 208

L

Larry's Shoes 315
Lemco Miller 305
Linda L. Miles
& Associates 232
Lord Publishing 206
Lynch, Ryan
& Associates 281

M

MacAcademy 51
Mackay Envelope 25
Macke Business
Products 88
MacTemps 21, 331
Magellan's 267
Manco 70, 105
MapInfo 294
MathSoft 304
MBS Communications 331
MDY Advanced
Technologies 278
Measurement
Specialties 107
Medical Graphics 341
Mona Meyer McGrath
& Gavin 328

Mother Myrick's 318
Mothers Work 316
Motor Cargo 173
MPR 141
M.R. Weiser & Co. 192, 255
Multiplex 110, 121, 327
Munchkin 43

N

National Commission
Against Drunk
Driving 286
National Computer
Security Assoc. 260
National Leadership
Coalition on AIDS 293
National Office Products
Assoc. 294
Natural Ovens
of Manitowoc 16
NCO Financial
Systems 303, 340
Negotiation Pro 18
Network Solutions 54
New Hope
Communications 138
New Pig 61
Norman Howe
& Associates 230
North American Tool
& Die 82
Nypro 244

O

Object Design 33
Offtech 118
Ogilvy Management 284
Oil Changers 132

Original Copy Centers 130
Outback Steakhouse 170

P

Pacific Bell 297
PacifiCare
Wellness 192, 224
Paric 201
PC Globe 50
Peabody & Brown 342
Peavey Electronics 163, 306
Pegasus Personal
Fitness 158
Penn Parking 171
Pentech International 20, 74
Performark 26
Personal Comfort Corp. 38
Pete's Brewing 16, 84
Phelps County Bank 58
PhotoWire 84
Physician Sales & Service 73
Premier Computer 126
Premiere
Merchandising 257
Pretty Neat Industries 81
Princeton Review 54
PROaudit 271
Pro Fasteners 178
PTI Environmental 266
Purgatory Resort 282

Q

QVC 38

R

Racing Strollers 225, 298
Rampell & Rampell 90
Real Goods Trading 209

Reflexite 210, 234, 247
Registry 141
Remediation Technologies 67
Renex 112
Research Frontiers 208
Rhino Foods 172, 199
Rocky Mountain
    Motorworks 215
Rosemary Macedonio
    & Associates 286
Rosenman & Colin 77, 291
Rue de France 26
Russian Information
    Services 52
R.W. Frookies 196

S

Saint Louis Bread Co. 190
San Luis Sourdough 97
Sandstrom Products 136
SBT Accounting
    Systems 300
Schmidt-Cannon 111
Sears 134
SecondWind 65
Sequent Computer
    Systems 176
Service Corps of Retired
    Executives 224
SET Laboratories 301
Sharon's Finest 224
Shawmut Design
    & Construction
    39, 193, 257
Silverman's 103
Skyline Displays 320
SkyRock 239
Soft Inc. 182

Softub 254
Solar Press 248
Specialized Bicycle
    Components 59
Sports Endeavors 263
Springfield Remanufacturing
    160, 202
Starbucks Coffee 37, 117
Stonyfield Farm 104
Sub Pop Records 37
Subway 128, 256
Sun Sportswear 200
Sundance Spas 198
Sunny Waterbeds 66
Super Market 76
Symphony Capital 279
Synopsys 181
SynOptics
    Communications 125

T

Tabra 180
Target 314
Technologic Partners 54
Tek-Aids Industries 253
Temps & Co. 313
Teubner & Associates 124
Texas Back Institute 337
Timecorp Systems 174
Timeslips 241
Trelltex 197
Triad LLC 154
Triton Marine Construction 62
Tusco Display 293

U

Unitech Composites 179
United Medical Resources 148

USA Global Link 217
U.S. Fitness Products 191
Utica National
    Insurance Group 273
UV Process Supply 99

V

Varet Marcus & Fink 212
Victorian Papers 184

W

Wall/Goldfinger 79
Walter Joseph
    Communications 154
Wellfleet
    Communications 125
Western NY Technology
    Development Center 245
Western Union Commercial
    Services 92
White Dog Cafe 93, 167
Wild Oats Market 124
Will-Burt 281
Winter Gardens Salad 156
Wisconsin Technicolor 205
Woodsmith 296
Woodworker's Supply 108
Work/Family Directions
    165, 275
Wright's Gourmet
    House 87, 149

Z

Zingerman's
    Delicatessen 164

Other business books from *Inc.* magazine

How to *Really* Create a Successful Business Plan
How to *Really* Start Your Own Business
How to *Really* Create a Successful Marketing Plan
By David E. Gumpert

How to *Really* Deliver Superior Customer Service
Edited by John Halbrooks

How to *Really* Recruit, Motivate, & Lead Your Team:
Managing People
Edited by Ruth G. Newman,
with Bradford W. Ketchum, Jr.

Anatomy of a Start-Up
Why Some New Businesses Succeed and Others Fail:
27 Real-life Case Studies
Edited by Elizabeth K. Longsworth

Managing People: 101 Proven Ideas for Making You
and Your People More Productive
From America's Smartest Small Companies
Edited by Sara P. Noble

To receive a complete listing of *Inc.* business
books and videos, please call 1-800-468-0800,
ext. 5007. Or write to *Inc.* Business Resources,
P.O. Box 1365, Dept. 5007, Wilkes-Barre, PA
18703-1365.